With Our Compliments

INSTITUTE FOR MANAGEMENT STUDIES

**Delivering Excellence in
Executive Education Since 1974**

**(775) 322-8222
www.ims-online.com**

Praise for *Make Up Your Mind*

"When you read a book that is so logical in the telling, you realize that this book is genius. It breaks down decision making into a very simple process that has helped me be a better consultant. I just use Hal's little business card reminders about what decision making is all about. I keep the card on the dashboard of my car and I refer to it before I visit any client. With this book now available, I will be able to refer people to a book that has powerful strength in helping keep us all on track and focused. It has been a helpful guide for me and I am sure it will be for others."

—**Lenard Bertrain, PhD**, Business Consultant

"Business leaders need to understand the basis of their decisions and how to optimize them. This book provides an effective framework that is brought to life with interesting anecdotes."

—**Garry E. Menzel, PhD**, Chief Operating Officer, Regulus Therapeutics

"Decision making, at all levels, is a major stumbling block for most companies to achieve their desired results of a transformation. *Make Up Your Mind* provides some incredibly practical ideas on how individuals and organizations can make better decisions. This book will help you to become a champion of fact-based, informed decision making in your life and in your organization."

—**Mark Holmstrom**, Chief Innovation Officer and Partner, Infosys Consulting

"With his book, *Make Up Your Mind*, Hal Mooz provides tools to assist everyone— from a student, to a parent, to a politician, to a Chief Executive—on how to achieve consistently better outcomes by making better decisions. This is a book you will want to read several times over, and buy multiple copies as gifts for those you care about."

—**Thomas J. Powell**, Chief Executive Officer, Resolute Capital Partners

"Hal's book brings discipline and structure to the sometimes daunting problem of choosing among alternatives in both simple and complex situations. *Make Up Your Mind* should assist anyone who faces choices in their business life as well as in their private life. The book provides clear examples of both situations and shows how the use of the techniques can result in focusing on defensible choices."

—**WEM**, Business Owner

"I have taught Decision Analysis for NASA and numerous aerospace and commercial organizations for over 20 years. I consider this book a valuable contribution to help organizations faced with technical decisions improve the processes they use and thus the decision outcomes that affect both business and mission success."

—**John R. Chiorini, PhD**, Business Consultant

"If you're lying awake at night, wondering how you'll tackle a high-impact decision, *Make Up Your Mind* provides a clear, concise approach. As has been noted before, common sense is rarely common knowledge. From deciding which projects to undertake, to managing the important decisions that occur throughout the project lifecycle, Hal provides a step-by-step technique to replace decision making that's all too often governed by 'gut feel' or intuition. I will recommend this book to all of our clients."

—**Dan Swaigen, PMP, MCP**, Chief Executive Officer, PM Connect, Inc.

"I've learned a lot while working with Hal Mooz over the years, such as how to listen, the real meaning of words and actions, and being proactively responsive to others. The challenge that has always been with me is what you are thinking, and now with his new book, the challenge is ever present! I think Hal brings it all home with *Make Up Your Mind!*"

—**Herb Myers**, Regional Business Banking, President, Wells Fargo & Co.

"We all want to make Good Decisions . . . yet often don't! Mooz's book *Make Up Your Mind* shows us how to do it better, and he highlights the many pitfalls we need to avoid along the way. He gives us a new way of thinking about this old process. A must-read for both home and business . . . and for both technical and nontechnical readers alike!"

—**Kevin Forsberg, PhD**, Expert Systems Engineering Professional and INCOSE Pioneer

"As a retired consulting economist, I am acutely aware of the uncertainties that surround forecasts and projections of economic and social behavior. I wish *Make up Your Mind* had been available to me, as I am sure it would have led me to more rigorously evaluate the uncertainties surrounding the bases for my recommendations and increase my clients' confidence in their possible outcomes."

—**Robert T. Mott**, Retired Consultant

"The great strength of this book lies not so much in its rigorous methodologies of decision making and analysis, but rather in the implied sense of ethics, integrity, and respect which the author champions for us. Even though his approach to decision making is 'modern' in its appeal to rigorous investigation, hard scientific evidence, and meticulous planning, it is actually very 'old-fashioned' in its commitment to the values of honor, responsibility, and personal integrity."

—**Jim Boyers, PhD**, Clinical Psychologist

"*Make Up Your Mind* is about choosing a decision. Mr. Mooz presents a manner, style, and a sustainable method of choosing for all the citizens of all ages of our world to utilize. Everyone will benefit by reading, studying, and absorbing this book."

—**Charles A. Arnold, MD**, Oncologist, Futures Pool Operator

"In this book, Hal Mooz has brought order to the process of decision making, more desperately needed here early in the twenty-first century than ever before in human history. The range of experience Mooz brings to the writing of a book about ways to make wise choices is extremely impressive as is the clarity and concreteness with which he sets forth the procedures he's devised. As a professor of English who for half a century has carefully examined the critical thinking skills of thousands of college students, I can testify to the desperate need for a book of this nature."

—**Jack Miles**, English Professor

MAKE UP
YOUR
MIND

ALSO BY HAL MOOZ

Visualizing Project Management: Models and Frameworks for Mastering Complex Systems, Third Edition (John Wiley & Sons, Inc., 2005)

Communicating Project Management: The Integrated Vocabulary of Project Management and Systems Engineering (John Wiley & Sons, Inc., 2003)

MAKE UP YOUR MIND

A Decision-Making
Guide to Thinking
Clearly and
Choosing Wisely

HAL MOOZ

WILEY

JOHN WILEY & SONS, INC.

Copyright © 2012 by Hal Mooz. All rights reserved.

Published by John Wiley & Sons, Inc., Hoboken, New Jersey.
Published simultaneously in Canada.

No part of this publication may be reproduced, stored in a retrieval system, or transmitted in any form or by any means, electronic, mechanical, photocopying, recording, scanning, or otherwise, except as permitted under Section 107 or 108 of the 1976 United States Copyright Act, without either the prior written permission of the Publisher, or authorization through payment of the appropriate per-copy fee to the Copyright Clearance Center, Inc., 222 Rosewood Drive, Danvers, MA 01923, (978) 750-8400, fax (978) 646-8600, or on the web at www.copyright.com. Requests to the Publisher for permission should be addressed to the Permissions Department, John Wiley & Sons, Inc., 111 River Street, Hoboken, NJ 07030, (201) 748-6011, fax (201) 748-6008, or online at http://www.wiley.com/go/permissions.

Limit of Liability/Disclaimer of Warranty: While the publisher and author have used their best efforts in preparing this book, they make no representations or warranties with respect to the accuracy or completeness of the contents of this book and specifically disclaim any implied warranties of merchantability or fitness for a particular purpose. No warranty may be created or extended by sales representatives or written sales materials. The advice and strategies contained herein may not be suitable for your situation. You should consult with a professional where appropriate. Neither the publisher nor author shall be liable for any loss of profit or any other commercial damages, including but not limited to special, incidental, consequential, or other damages.

For general information on our other products and services or for technical support, please contact our Customer Care Department within the United States at (800) 762-2974, outside the United States at (317) 572-3993 or fax (317) 572-4002.

Wiley publishes in a variety of print and electronic formats and by print-on-demand. Some material included with standard print versions of this book may not be included in e-books or in print-on-demand. If this book refers to media such as a CD or DVD that is not included in the version you purchased, you may download this material at http://booksupport.wiley.com. For more information about Wiley products, visit www.wiley.com.

Library of Congress Cataloging-in-Publication Data:

Mooz, Hal.
   Make up your mind : a decision-making guide to thinking clearly and choosing wisely / Hal Mooz.
     p.   cm.
   Includes bibliographical references and index.
   ISBN 978-1-118-17271-1 (cloth); ISBN 978-1-118-22688-9 (ebk);
ISBN 978-1-118-22973-6 (ebk); ISBN 978-1-118-22955-2 (ebk)
     1. Decision making.   2. Thought and thinking.   I. Title.
   BF448.M66   2012
   153.8'3—dc23

                                                                2011037182

Printed in the United States of America
10 9 8 7 6 5 4 3 2 1

A good decision can have good or bad outcome
A bad decision can have good or bad outcome
All decisions may be unknowingly permanently recorded
How then do we achieve the outcomes that we desire and
are proud of?

CONTENTS

WHY THIS BOOK?

This book is directed toward all segments of our population. It was created to help readers become skilled in thinking more clearly about their decisions and in applying appropriate judgments to make actionable choices. While the included models are helpful for decisions of low impact, they are most useful for decisions of significance that often cause anxiety, stress, and loss of sleep. The rational step-by-step methods for framing both the decision type and the potential solutions and in valuing the decision alternatives will usually lead to the best choice.

Businesspeople will find it helpful in leading their decision processes at work. Families will be able to arrive at better consensus-based conclusions. Inquisitive teenagers will benefit by making more informed decisions about their education, career, and lifestyle. Everyone can benefit by becoming decision fit. These principles can help meet that goal.

FOREWORD

Making good decisions is a crucial skill at every level.

—Peter Drucker[1]

Decision: de•ci•sion (n.)[2]

1. The passing of judgment on an issue under consideration.
2. The act of reaching a conclusion or making up one's mind.
3. A conclusion or judgment reached or pronounced; a verdict.

We all make decisions every day and I suspect that most of us don't consider the process we use to determine each decision. Decisions can be as routine as selecting something to wear or to eat, or as complicated as choosing a career or making a life-altering medical decision.

Decisions we make reflect much of who we are. Executives and managers expect their colleagues to know how to make well-founded and defensible decisions. We expect our government representatives to make logical decisions when acting on behalf of constituents. Our families expect us to make decisions in the best interest of the family. Parents struggle with teaching their children how to make sensible decisions that will affect their futures in a positive

---

[1] *Harvard Business Review*, June 1, 2004.
[2] *The Free Dictionary* by Farlex.

way. Yet in the face of these expectations and challenges, decision making is typically not taught without pursuing elective training in decision making.

What is a good decision and how do we learn to make better decisions? Ask a room full of people and you will get a variety of answers. Seasoned decision makers will agree that with experience we learn to make better choices, but along the way most of us would admit we learn from the "school of hard knocks." When we make bad decisions we hope to learn from them and move on to make better decisions over time. However, in this age of digital permanence with YouTube, Facebook, and a myriad of other networks, the recording of our bad decisions can remain intact to haunt us for a very long time. This alone should encourage each of us to seek training to help make better decisions.

This book is a practical guide to thinking clearly about decisions and what is at stake with any decision. It identifies four aspects of serious decisions that are rarely consciously considered. Can the decision result in a very bad outcome? Will the outcome be permanent? Does the outcome result in a binding agreement with others? Will the judgment be based on certain or uncertain information?

Decision choices are based on our best judgment. However, we are rarely conscious of what our best judgment is based on. This book identifies and describes the 10 bases for passing judgment on decision alternatives, all of which are found in daily practice. Some bases are defensible and some are not, depending on the decision at hand. The author includes a powerful decision judgment model that can serve as a valuable reminder and should improve the basis of your future decision judgments.

While logic-based decisions are widely publicized in books and magazines, the author of *Make Up Your Mind* offers five proven processes, each adding increased precision, resulting in more sound and defensible outcomes.

Paradigm shifts occur when you no longer think and believe as you once did and you adopt a new view of an old standard. This book is sure to shift one or more paradigms about how you and others make decisions.

I trust you will believe as I do that this book is long overdue and will help future decision makers become decision fit.

—**Jeff Henley**
Chairman, Oracle Corporation

BACKGROUND AND ACKNOWLEDGMENTS

In 2005, my company was selected to partner with Stanford University's Professional Development Program in the creation and delivery of a certificate program in Systems Engineering. My background as a Lockheed Chief Systems Engineer and my experience in training thousands of systems engineers made this a logical fit. Our Stanford partner was Dr. Ron Howard, internationally recognized and often quoted as the expert on decision analysis. Since project management and systems engineering require skilled decision making this was a mutually reinforcing partnership. At the time I could not envision how my outlook on life and business practices would change.

The curriculum development required ongoing interactions for the sharing of ideas. While we were discussing with Dr. Howard the importance of baseline management to systems engineering, he was educating us on the details of making decisions based on difficult to quantify uncertainty. It was an environment of mutual discovery and learning.

Early in my systems engineering career I benefited from formal training in multiattribute fact-based decision making, which is considerably different from Dr. Howard's major interest of decisions made based on uncertainty. In my development of space systems my objective was to reduce uncertainty to near zero through research and experimentation bolstered by robust designs that were fault tolerant to handle inevitable uncertainties. So while Dr. Howard's excellent work was meaningful, in many instances it was not directly relevant to me based on my systems engineering experience.

Dr. Howard's influence caused me to become decision aware. That is, I began to observe others, including those reported by the media, making many flawed decisions. Root cause analysis of these bad decisions revealed that there are many bases for decision judgment, some of which are good, and defensible, and others that—although popular—can lead to flawed and nondefensible outcomes. This triggered two actions on my part. I proceeded to read the available books on decision making and simultaneously I began noting the decision judgment bases that decision makers used. Concurrently I began incorporating decision making into my project management and systems engineering training to benefit from student feedback, which is always beneficial.

Several years of research into published work on decision making revealed that there was no consistent way of categorizing the type of decision being made (what is at stake) and there was no well accepted model of the many bases for making decision judgment. Both of these are provided in this book.

I want to thank Dr. Ronald Howard for awakening my passion for the subject of decision making. Since then it has been difficult for me to think of anything else. I also thank Dr. Colonel Anthony Rizzo who introduced me to the concept of permanent errors; those for which you can only apologize but cannot change the outcome.

In the development of this book and an associated training course I often engaged colleagues for brutally frank feedback. I want to thank Dr. Kevin Forsberg, Ken Mosteller, Dr. John Chiorini, Jim Whalen, Bill Flury, Dr. Joe Keogh, Dan Swaigen, and Bill Van Vleet for their unvarnished feedback.

In addition, I tapped into a diverse set of business executives for their perspectives. I want to thank Herb Myers, Roger Fuller, Dave House, Dr. Charles Arnold, Carol Arnold, Tom Powell, and Don Putterman for their valuable influence.

Dr. Rick Giarrusso and Dr. Thomas Seyller, both with PhDs in Decision Analysis under Dr. Howard, confirmed that my material was unique, original, and worthwhile and that I should continue with the development.

Herb Myers introduced me to Dr. Leonard Bertrain, another consultant and nonfiction author, who has provided valuable insight and feedback.

I received valuable input and editing advice from John Miles, and Bob Mott. They helped make the material professional and readable. I am grateful for their assistance.

A special thank you to Lauren Murphy, my ongoing John Wiley & Sons editor who, after some convincing, got the Wiley team enthusiastic about championing this book into the business marketplace.

I especially appreciate that my wife, Constance Heldman, who has always supported the idea of this book and provided continuous valuable input and urged me on in spite of periodic mental blocks. We both believe this work is important, especially for the younger individuals about to make important decisions that will affect the rest of their lives. We will be developing a book oriented to young people to help them make better quality-of-life decisions.

May your life benefit from better decision outcomes because of your improved decision fitness.

PREFACE

We live in an age where healthy living and physical fitness are all the rage. Media of all types promote improving our physical well-being through a healthy lifestyle. But conspicuous by its absence is any encouragement to become decision fit so that we can deliberately make the best choices in our personal and business lives. Although our daily decisions largely determine whether we achieve the success we desire, we are seldom trained in this most important of skills. This book will help you think clearly about decisions, their outcomes, and the 10 bases of judgment that you are free to apply every time you make a choice. Some are apt to get you into trouble while others will help achieve your objectives. By becoming decision fit you will give yourself the best shot at making the right choices. The world needs more decision-fit people who know how to properly apply the appropriate judgment methods. Congratulations on striving to become one of these people. Now when you are pressured to make up your mind you will enjoy new confidence in doing so based on thinking clearly about the challenge and the solution.

The premise of this book is that *clarity of thought* leads to *effective action, the desired outcome of any decision*. However, because unclear thinking often exists when making the most basic of decisions, many decisions are poorly formulated and poorly executed, resulting in unintended consequences that can be irrevocably life shaping. We live in an age of digital permanence. Our decisions are often unknowingly or even knowingly recorded, sometimes to our embarrassment. We may be recorded by video cameras during our daily routine or digitized as we conduct business with e-mails, texting, and photo and video exchanging, all of which produce indelible digital histories. We must be purposely diligent in our decision making to achieve our intended objectives; at the same time, we must be self-disciplined in order to avoid undermining our future with thoughtless actions that can plague our reputations and detour us from our preferred course. The concepts in this book are directed at producing better outcomes by achieving clarity of thought and taking effective actions based on that thinking.

Why does clarity of thinking matter? "How you think is how you act is how you are. The way you think creates the results you get. The most powerful way to improve the quality of your results is to improve the way you think" (Haines).

This book is about improving the clarity of thinking about decisions.

Making good decisions is fundamental to one's personal and business success. Yet most of us pass through life never deliberately developing this critical skill. Our fuzzy thinking leads to unwise choices and undesirable outcomes. How else does one explain buying a car based on what is currently "in style" only to find it doesn't satisfy our needs? Or selecting a cute dog only to find it at the bottom of the intelligence list and not trainable? Or buying sugar-loaded snack food because we are impressed by the "no fat" label and mistakenly interpret it to mean "nonfattening"? Far more important, when the world's situation is critically examined it is obviously fraught with the results of poorly made decisions that will continue to impact societies for generations to come. (Consider foreign policies, war, economic tactics, etc.) Our personal lives, our business choices, and critical global issues beg for the application of sound decision making that is rooted in logic, based on facts, and is consistent with high standards of morals and ethics.

Despite the abundance of books and published papers on decision analysis and decision making, many tend to focus on the mathematics associated with decisions made in the presence of uncertainty and quickly apply statistical probability to arrive at a best choice. But then these same experts often warn of the risks of the choice; the human inability to remain objective, to accurately estimate probabilities and their impacts, and to be rational and unbiased in applying known facts. *Make Up Your Mind* is not about applying precise mathematics to fuzzy probabilities to arrive at a suspect answer. Instead it is about selecting and properly applying the most appropriate basis and processes for making decisions of all types.

While this book will introduce you to many sound decision-making methods and processes, other books and courses offer increased depth into decision processes of interest.

Many of the included examples of decisions are from the author's experiences as well as those found in the daily press. With public examples so prevalent, it's clear that bad decisions plague our planet. With decision-making education we can improve our decision-making skills and become a population of decision-fit decision makers.

PART

I

Are You Decision Fit?

Decision Environment

Introduction

The question, "What were you thinking?" has been popularized by Dr. Phil McGraw of the *Dr. Phil Show*. Show participants are often challenged with this specific question in an attempt to explain how they arrived at a mental state so bizarre that they're willing to appear on national television to serve as a dramatic and negative learning example to millions of viewers. We witness it all: eating disorders, sexual misconduct, addictions, violence, corporate misconduct, dishonesty, deception, you name it. And in every case the decisions leading to these notorious outcomes were deliberately selected by the perpetrators when more beneficial alternatives were available. So what were these people thinking when they made these decisions?

Even though Dr. Phil almost always raises this critical question, he rarely receives an answer from his guests. In most cases his query remains unanswered. Consequently viewers fail to learn from the flawed thinking and inappropriate choices that led to the conditions on exhibit.

This book is about becoming skillful enough that sound decision making becomes so second nature that the appropriate judgment basis is selected and confidently and proficiently applied. In short, it's about becoming "decision fit." That is, being qualified and skilled in all aspects of making decisions, ranging from low to high significance as well as those with differing degrees of relevant information uncertainty.

I have become highly decision aware and notice flawed decisions almost every day. When this happens, I often think, "What was he

5

or she thinking?" And, "Why wasn't a more appropriate decision process applied?"

My very bright friend John had a successful year and decided to treat his wife to a new SUV. As he drove it past me on his return from the dealership I immediately thought, "What is he thinking?" I had just read in *Consumer Reports* that the vehicle he selected was on the magazine's "The Worst of the Worst" list, which included the worst reliability record of all vehicles. As might be expected, over the next several months the vehicle was in the shop being repaired more than it was being enjoyed by John's wife. At one point John exclaimed, "One more fault and I am invoking the California Lemon Law!"

The Lemon Law requires that if the manufacturer, or its representative such as an authorized dealer, is unable to service or repair a new motor vehicle to meet the terms of an express written warranty after a reasonable number of repair attempts, the manufacturer is required to replace the vehicle or return the purchase price to the lessee or buyer.

My avocation of building and renovating homes prompts me to observe what others are doing in construction. Recently I watched two very large and heavy homes being built on the surface of extremely soft, highly compressible fill without piers driven to bedrock to stabilize them. It is well known by the residents of this community that settling will surely occur, resulting in fractured foundations and tilted homes. So what were the designers, engineers, builders, and inspectors thinking? They saved less than 2 percent of the building cost by not incorporating the better solution of piers driven to bedrock as others in the same area have done. When these homes require re-leveling it will cost more than the amount saved and it will have to be done multiple times over the life of the structure. In addition, if these owners decide to market their home for sale, by law they must disclose to potential buyers the risk of settling and the associated re-leveling that is sure to deter some potential buyers.

Most people are familiar with the flawed launch decision of the *Challenger* space shuttle. The *Challenger* decision is referenced several times here because it is a famous, fully recorded, and well-analyzed decision that was made badly and caused seven astronauts to die. We can learn much from it.

It is traditional in the space business to prove that the predicted environmental launch conditions are safe (essentially benign) for a mission launch. Prelaunch discussions focus on the required margin of safety to permit a "Go for launch" decision. In the case of the *Challenger*, based on the Rodger's Commission Failure Report and the ABC reenactment derived from that report, the NASA/Thiokol discussions relative to the Thiokol Solid Rocket Boosters transitioned from "Will it be safe?" to "Can you prove that it will fail?" rather than having to prove the *Challenger* would not fail. What were the management personnel thinking when deciding it was okay to launch into untested environmental conditions against their experts' recommendations? There are opinions that the launch went ahead in order to get a higher performance rating (a financial perk) from NASA, which would be lower if they had changed the launch date for warmer temperatures.

Years later, on the international scene, the world became convinced that Iraq possessed weapons of mass destruction (WMD; nuclear, chemical, and/or biological weapons). Multiple inspection teams failed to find WMD evidence but the senior decision makers were convinced of their existence because of a lone informant (code-named "Curveball") and the expectation that the WMDs would eventually be located. Based on no hard evidence from multiple inspection teams, but very strong intuition and the word of the single informant, the Iraq War was approved. As we are now aware, no evidence of WMD was ever found and the informant has since confessed to fabricating the story. So, what were the decision makers thinking?

The investigation into the destruction of the Fukushima nuclear power plant subsequent to the March 2011 Japanese earthquake-caused tsunami has revealed that the design engineers elected to ignore worst case earthquake and tsunami predictions and instead adopted much less severe conditions as their driving design environment. As a result, reactor clustering and reduced plant fortification were accepted as satisfactory. The outcome of these flawed decisions will be felt for years.

The business section of our newspapers occasionally cites instances of corporate executives back-dating stock options without proper financial disclosure or puffing up the financial appearance of their companies to inflate company performance and therefore their stock prices. Since these are violations of both the law and business ethics, what were these executives thinking when they ordered these improper actions?

The previous examples illustrate how pervasive flawed decision making is within our society and how it can lead to significant negative and often permanent consequences. It is done at the individual level, the family level, the corporate level, and the national level. The reason it's so common is that, like the critical skill of parenting, decision-making skills are typically not taught in our formative years. Hence, we learn it by osmosis and by trial and error, unless we deliberately add it to our skill set through specialized elective study.

In practice, snap judgment is sometimes applied to critical decisions. This happened in the decision to land the *Columbia* shuttle even though NASA knew a large piece of insulation probably struck the wing on launch and that they could have taken damage assessment photographs while in flight. Responsible foam engineer experts requested to investigate possible damage to the wing after viewing video clips that showed the probable foam impact with the shuttle wing leading edge. However, the suspect damage was quickly proclaimed by a NASA executive, known for snap decisions, to be merely a routine maintenance problem to be repaired after landing. She declined to support the expert's request to gather confirming data that was available by requesting damage assessment photographs to be taken from a photographic satellite operated by another government agency. Her intuition and the supporting intuition of other NASA officials, without specific foam expertise, was that the lightweight foam would disintegrate on impact with the rigid structure of the orbiter and would not cause damage. The *Columbia* disintegrated on reentry when atmospheric gasses penetrated the damaged wing, causing complete structural failure. Subsequent simulation tests proved that lightweight foam impacting the wing at high velocity would and did shatter the leading edge of the wing, a counterintuitive outcome. *Intuition is risky when the laws of physics rule and the stakes are high.*

Teenagers often make critical quality-of-life choices without realizing what they've done. Major decisions like dropping out of school or using illegal drugs are often based on emotion or peer pressure without considering the potential consequences to their future. Many teenage decisions are permanent, irrevocable, and can affect quality of life forever. Teen pregnancy, illegal drug use, Internet postings, and gang membership are examples.

Important decisions deserve appropriate analysis. But what is appropriate?

Sometimes analysis paralyzes simple choices, as when a waiter must revisit a dinner group multiple times because one person is unable to make a simple meal selection. Conversely, sometimes snap decisions are made without proper consideration of the seriousness of potential outcomes. We were led to believe that the Iraq people would greet our troops with flowers. They didn't. There should be sufficient decision analysis to provide confidence that the correct decision is being addressed, that the relevant facts are available, and that the correct judgment basis will be applied using a credible process.

We need to train ourselves to be able to gauge the significance of decisions and assess their consequences. Once a decision is properly defined and categorized then the appropriate analyses and judgment basis can be decided and applied.

This book addresses common misunderstandings and flaws prevalent in decision making and provides clarity, vocabulary, and decision processes that can guide you and your teams to better decisions. After becoming "decision fit" you will become acutely aware of sound decision making and you will have a new appreciation for those who know how to make good decisions. You will also become tuned in to poor decision making and you may feel sufficiently empowered to intervene and guide others when appropriate.

If a single decision-fit person had been part of the *Challenger* launch decision group it's likely he or she would have brought to the team's attention that they'd thoughtlessly jumped from expert-based judgment, to fact-based, to doctrine-based, to intuition-based decision judgment. And then tragically they succumbed to a pressure-based decision in order to justify their overriding objective: to launch no matter what the conditions. No one on either the NASA or Thiokol decision teams recognized their journey down this slippery slope that led to the ultimate disaster, the death of seven astronauts.

Decisions Shape Your Future

We face and make decisions from the time we are born. While we get parental guidance for a period of time it's not long before we're making decisions on our own: the food we like or dislike, whether to cry or not, to smile or not, and what toys we like. While we don't understand how we make these decisions they represent our first on-the-job training.

Without formal decision training we enter the preteen years, where we begin to make decisions crucially significant for our future: decisions about friends, interests, styles, hobbies, sports, music, passions, religion. Some of the decision outcomes will be part of our lives forever. Subconsciously, we make decisions relative to our relationship with our parents, our credibility, and our personality. Yet when we make these life-influencing decisions we make them without understanding the method we are applying, or the possible consequences. We would do well to train preteens in decision making to prepare them for these life-shaping choices.

Rarely do teenagers realize the critical importance of the decisions made during this phase of their lives. It's a time when parental and peer pressure is greatest, and seldom is peer pressure in the best interests of the teen's long-term potential. Teenagers will decide whether to stay in or drop out of school, do their best or just get by, join a gang, use illegal drugs, engage in sexual activity, seek further education, join a fraternity, and a host of other potentially life-shaping decisions. Millions of young people, without knowledgeable adults to help, face these decisions when they're often ill-equipped to make them. Unfortunately, mentoring adults (if available) may be equally unskilled in decision making. This deficiency often leads to flawed judgment and poor selections.

My wife volunteers and mentors youth at the Boys and Girls Club of America. Her work often involves facilitating discussions between youth, parents, and high school counselors. It's not unusual for her to find that neither the youths nor their parents know what questions to pursue to gather the required information to make informed decisions about the aspects of pursuing higher education. The training of high school students in decision making should be a high priority for the directors of our education system.

Adult decisions span the range from the very personal to those that affect others, and we often make dozens daily. Unfortunately, we normally apply the same methods that we learned "on-the-job" as teenagers, leading to decisions that are incorrectly valued and poorly expressed. This is often followed by improper basis of judgment and an incorrectly applied judgment process almost invariably leading to flawed choices. It is always surprising to me that thousands of people purchase products that have been condemned by both rating organizations and by the product users that post their negative experiences on the Web. Why would anyone frequent a one-star restaurant with unsanitary ratings?

We should all accept the personal responsibility to become decision fit and capable of reliably making good decisions.

Many of us are familiar with the embarrassing decision outcomes of the Edsel automobile, the "new" Coke, Betamax, and the fiber optic glut of the last decade. All of these were products of decision making that failed to validate the market and confirm both the need and the customer demand before committing to full-scale deployment. As you might expect, countless other products have similar tales of failing to meet promised expectations.

Business and technical environments are faced with a myriad of decisions. As a chief systems engineer I was responsible for decisions regarding requirements, concepts, specifications, verification, validation, qualification, and deployment. Restaurant owners must decide on location, ambiance, menu, pricing, suppliers, staffing, and so forth. Physicians must decide on the seriousness of symptoms, tests required, treatment required, prescriptions and doses, emergency actions, and more. A common factor of most business decisions is that they must be defensible to oversight by management, partners, funding organizations, customers, and government agencies that have the power of critical review and audit. Not all judgment bases can stand up to critical assessment. A decision-fit person will know how to succeed in an oversight audit.

Decision Fundamentals for Thinking Clearly

Before proceeding into the concepts and processes of decision-fit decision making there are fundamentals related to decision making that are not always intuitive and are important to making decisions of all kinds. What follows are significant truths that underlie good decision making. Some may surprise and even challenge you to shift a paradigm or two.

Decision Rigor Is Driven by the Fear of a Negative Outcome

Decisions of low consequence—like selecting a beverage, a meal, or a book to read—have very little potential of disappointing in any significant way. These decisions are easy to make and we rarely lose sleep or become anxious over the chance of a bad outcome with these decisions. Conversely, decisions like marriage, career, surgery, and investments have the potential of a large downside to our well-being and it is common for us to agonize over them because of the fear of the worst possible outcome. Decisions of minor consequence can be made with very little rigor but decisions with the potential for highly undesirable outcomes are worthy of rigorous process to ensure the best choice. This book will help you determine the appropriate rigor.

Intentions, Decisions, and Outcomes

How would you define a decision? Most people believe that they have made a decision when they proclaim that they have decided to stop smoking, lose weight, change employment, go to school, and the like. However, until the decision-related action is taken these are only intentions. The distinction between an intention and a decision is the decision action to achieve the intention.

It is interesting and important to recognize that *individuals will usually judge themselves by their best intentions* even though the intentions may never get implemented by the triggering action. In sharp contrast, *people will usually judge others by their worst action*. As an example, think about which action President Bill Clinton, a Rhodes Scholar, is most famous for. His good work has been overwhelmed by a significant bad permanent decision in which his affair with Monica Lewinsky became his career's worst credential. He can never erase the notoriety earned by "it depends on what the definition of 'is' is."

Some decision analysis experts define a decision as "an irrevocable allocation of resources." The example used is that if you purchase something such as a car and then decide later that you don't want it you will suffer a loss of money (resources) when you sell it as a used car, demonstrating a loss of resources by the decision action to complete the purchase. I believe that this definition is not always true and I offer a different perspective.

If I decide to lose weight and I take the action to skip a few meals I have made a clear decision including the implementing action and in doing so I have not irrevocably allocated resources. In fact, in this example the opposite has occurred, as I have preserved resources by not spending them on the unconsumed meals. Decision actions do not necessarily consume resources.

Any decision is a selection between two or more alternatives. To make the selection, comparative judgment of the alternatives is appropriate. A sound definition of a decision is *applying judgment to select an alternative and act on it*. This leads to the following definition of a good decision.

Definition of a Good Decision

The definition of a good decision that is relevant to the remainder of this book is: A good decision is applying informed judgment based on relevant facts (the head factor) and quality ethics (the heart factor) to select an alternative and to act on it.

A good decision selects the alternative with the best chance of achieving the desired outcome *given the information available at the time*. Decision processes, which are illustrated later, provide judgment guidance helpful in achieving an appropriate selection.

Good and Bad Decisions and Outcomes

How would you define a good decision? When conducting classroom training on decision making we challenge the class with this question. The overwhelmingly predictable response is that "a good decision is one that has a good outcome." This view is so prevalent that a recently published book on making decisions declares that you cannot determine the quality of a decision for two years as you evaluate the outcome over time. While this definition sounds perfectly logical, it is flawed and misleading.

To illustrate, an individual can insist on driving someone home while drunk and succeed in doing so without an accident. In this example a bad (illegal) decision was made to drive while under the influence and the designated driver overruled this decision and safely delivered the passenger home, which is a good outcome. Conversely, one can stay strictly sober as the designated driver and experience a serious accident while driving home. In the second example it was a good decision to remain sober but the good decision did not prevent a bad outcome. Unforeseen circumstances altered the outcome. This is an important distinction since external, unpredictable factors can influence good, well-informed decisions and result in bad outcomes. Unfortunately many television sports reporters fail to realize this distinction and often conclude that bad sports outcomes (results) are the result of bad decisions and criticize them as such. Investment decisions are also often unfairly judged by their ultimate outcome rather than the logic of initially making the investment selection.

The preceding examples demonstrate a decision making fundamental: good decisions can have good or bad outcomes and bad decisions can have good or bad outcomes; but, *good decisions have a much higher probability of good outcomes*. The methods provided in this book will markedly increase your potential of making good decisions.

Decision Making and Sunk Costs

Many decisions are made incorrectly because of the perceived influence of sunk costs. In business situations it is not uncommon to hear a decision influencer proclaim, "We cannot cancel this project; we have invested too much to cancel it." Or an investor will state, "I cannot sell this stock until it recovers to my purchase price."

In my training class we pose the following dilemma.

You recently spent $40,000 for a sports car that you are very proud of. However, you are about to close on a new house and need the money invested in the car to afford the house down payment so your car must be sold.

Should what you paid for the car influence the amount you are willing to sell the car for?

The answer of course is that the value of anything has nothing to do with the original price or cost but rather the current market value, where a willing buyer and a willing seller come to terms on a fair price. Yet in spite of this truth, companies will continue to fund low value projects because of the large amounts they have already invested, which they are reluctant to write off as a bad outcome of a decision.

A decision maker facing the impact of sunk costs may have to admit a mistake and recommend the cancellation of a project or product. Since this can be damaging to one's career, it is human nature to perpetuate an unsuccessful situation beyond its useful life.

To deal more effectively with situations where sunk cost is likely to influence the objectivity of the decision maker, a new decision maker should be applied that has no vested interest in the project's past history and is concerned only with the current and potential value of continuing to a probable conclusion.

This approach is also useful where status quo of projects and/or products tends to be preferred over emerging new concepts. A fresh and objective assessment is often needed to cause a paradigm shift in thinking about embedded projects and products.

Decision Making and the Cost/Price of Indifference

When making decisions that include the purchase or sale of anything it is important to understand the concept of the Cost/Price of Indifference. In a buying decision the cost of indifference is the highest amount that you are willing to pay and at that price you will be equally happy whether you consummate the transaction or if you do not. You will be emotionally indifferent. As an example, if you decide to bid on an item on eBay, bidding early is counterproductive and only serves to escalate the price progression. Instead, you should determine your price of indifference, which is the price at which you will experience the same emotional state whether you win or lose the bidding competition. You then enter that bid just prior to the end of the bidding period and if you win below that amount you will be pleased but if someone outbids you, you will not experience remorse for not bidding higher. Bidders who fail to adhere to this tactic often spend hours repeatedly tracking and bidding only to wish that they had bid a little higher when not successful. Similar tactics apply to selling an item. You can set your minimum bid (reserve) at your price of indifference and any bid above that will please you but a sale at your minimum or no sale will be emotionally satisfactory to you.

Two Decision-Making Stages

There are two major stages to making good decisions. The first stage is getting the decision statement, the decision type frame, and the decision solution frame correct. The second phase is the judging of which alternative best satisfies the decision statement based on the solution frame judgment criterion. This is illustrated in Figure 2.1. Each of these steps will be fully defined.

The Impact of the Decision Outcome

Decision significance is a personal assessment that involves both the tolerance for risk and the assessment of the impact of the potential negative consequences. Bill Gates, one of the world's richest people, can invest 10 or 20 thousand dollars without adversely risking his standard of living, while a person with little savings would find risking 10 or 20 thousand dollars a decision having a very significant potential negative impact. Decision significance is a measure of the personal tolerance for the potential negative outcomes influenced by the adequacy of relevant decision information. If there is the potential of a highly negative outcome and the decision must be based on highly uncertain information it is a decision of high significance. Life and death medical decisions are often in this category.

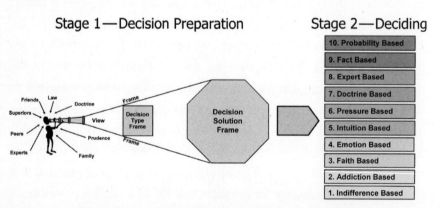

Figure 2.1   Two Decision-Making Stages.

Decision Maker's Viewpoint

Establishing the correct viewpoint of the decision maker is the first step to making a good decision (see Figure 2.2). Unfortunately it is one of the most difficult, as various stakeholders must be accommodated, especially those with a large amount of influence and who also may not be an advocate of the process. In making business decisions the legally and ethically driven stakeholders should weigh heavily on influencing the decision statement, objectives, and decision solution frame.

The adult decision maker may be influenced by the illustrated forces and their issues. Yet in considering and responding to these forces the decision maker must be mindful of pursuing a prudent solution.

The viewpoint of a teenager in making life-defining decisions is something close to the illustration in Figure 2.3 if the teen is being diligent about decision making. Some teens will seek out and accept guidance from their elders while others will keep their distance and demonstrably defy adult advice. Unfortunately, some teens are mainly emotion or peer pressure driven (or both) and will not involve any enlightened stakeholders who could guide them away from making bad choices.

Stakeholder influence can shape the view that the decision maker adopts in formulating the decision to be decided. For example, if a teen is deciding on a college to attend, a friend with a rave review

Figure 2.2   Adult Decision Maker's Viewpoint.

Figure 2.3 Teen Decision Maker's Viewpoint.

about a favored fraternity can influence the teen's decision to make sure their college choices include that fraternity.

The Boys and Girls Club of America's College Bound Program and KIPP (Knowledge Is Power Program) Charter Schools are dedicated to influencing young underserved student decision makers to establish a college education as a life decision and to take the necessary preparatory actions early to ensure achievement of that goal. They have achieved amazing success in causing these youth to seek lofty educational goals.

Decision Fitness

Decision fitness has been mentioned but not yet defined. To be decision fit one must be proficient at the following:

- Specifying the decision and context
- Determining the decision type
- Creating the decision type frame
- Developing the decision solution frame
- Creating viable alternatives
- Identifying and getting the comparative information
- Knowledgably selecting the right judgment basis
- Skillfully applying the appropriate judgment process

- Effectively managing power and peer pressure
- Objectively making the judgment
- Decisively implementing the action

Decision Fatigue

Research has shown that decision fitness and the ability to reliably make sound judgments can be strongly influenced by both recent decision intensity and the decision maker's nourishment resulting in decision fatigue. Decision fatigue has been proven to be experienced as a result of making many decisions in close succession typical of business and shopping environments. As the quantity of decisions mount it is human nature to relax the rigor of upcoming decisions often relinquishing the judgment to the default mode or to the adoption of judgment by indifference. Retailers are keenly aware of this condition. They know that the aisle after aisle shopping experience causes decision fatigue and they deliberately surround their checkout stations with products that are subject to emotional impulse buying that would normally be countered by rational thinking, but the brain is too fatigued to apply rational analysis.

Research has also shown that decision rigor also decreases with reducing glucose levels. Decisions made early in the day, just following lunch, and after an afternoon break including snack food, benefit from increased analysis and logical thinking while decisions made with reduced glucose levels are treated more superficially and are relegated to the status quo or default mode. This is particularly serious when prisoners are up for parole and the early birds win parole and the late comers with identical conditions are denied the same parole opportunity since the decision fatigued parole board members opt for the easy and safe decision to maintain the status quo.

The Decision Type Frame

Crafting the Decision Statement

The decision statement should be prepared and sufficiently challenged to ensure that it correctly represents the dilemma to be resolved. As an example, "What car should I buy?" might be the initial conceived decision. A challenge can be made of the word "car" since it precludes consideration of other forms of vehicles. When modified to "What vehicle should I buy?" it will include SUVs, trucks, crossovers, and so forth. It can then be further challenged since buying precludes the alternatives of leasing and renting. When further modified to, "What vehicle should I acquire?" it can then be further challenged to "What transportation should I use?" and even "Do I need to travel?" If these statements do not represent the desired objective then the statement should be adjusted to the most representative statement. In this example it might be "What vehicle should I acquire?"

Sometimes the wrong decision is addressed. I had the occasion to help a teen make an important decision. The teen wanted to take a dance class elective but the added class would replace a study period, depriving him of homework time. He could not decide whether to take the dance class or not. During my interview he revealed that his life ambition was to own a dance studio and teach others. I suggested that taking the dance class would significantly contribute to that ambition and his decision should be "Am I willing to convert an hour of TV time or computer game time to homework that would then replace the lost study period time that would be consumed by the dance class?" He discovered that the reframed decision was much easier to handle and happily signed up for the dance elective.

The wording of the decision statement can shape the outcomes in a significant way. Ballot propositions are often worded to achieve the outcomes the ballot writer desires. The following old story illustrates this point.

Two monks who were heavy smokers would often smoke and pray together. They became concerned that their smoking was a sin and decided to ask their superiors for guidance. When they met the next day one was puffing away when the second arrived and exclaimed, "The head of the monastery told me it is a sin." "What did you ask him?" said the first. "I asked him if it was all right to smoke during our evening prayer, and he said no." "Well," said the smoking monk, "I asked if it was all right to pray during our evening smoke, and he said it was just fine."

Another illustration comes from research that shows the importance of decision wording. The revealing exercise challenged various groups to decide on Drug A or Drug B per the following scenario.

There are two new miracle drugs to cure a fatal disease that produce the following results:

If Drug A is used 60 percent of users will survive.

If Drug B is used 40 percent of users will die.

Even though these outcomes are identical there is an overwhelming preference for Drug A because of the more positive-sounding alternative.

Propositions presented to the voting public are often worded in a way that a yes vote is a denial and a no vote is an approval.

There are now *Choice Architects*, who carefully word the selections for you to choose from. You see evidence of a Choice Architect's work any time there are default settings on electronic devices and when you are considering options on insurance forms, 401(k) plans, and in voting booths. The Choice Architect is a master at wording to achieve the intended outcome of the sponsor.

Decisions usually involve many stakeholders, some with significant equity and high interest in the outcome. While challenging for the decision maker, consensus should be achieved on the decision statement among all significant stakeholders. This important step is part of being decision fit. The extent and thoroughness of the decision definition should correlate to the decision significance and the basis for judgment. For instance, if your decision is of low significance and the judgment is to be indifference based, the statement need not be as comprehensive as a decision of higher significance. However, if the decision is of high significance to you and is to be fact-based or probability-based, then the decision definition should be comprehensive, including criteria profiles representing the values of the decision maker and those of the heavy hitting stakeholders. Since fact-based and probability-based decisions require the most accurate decision definitions, they will be explained in Chapter 4, leaving rightsizing and adjustment of less rigorous decision bases to the reader.

The Decision Context

Context refers to the conditions and circumstances that are relevant to an event or fact. Decision makers must know the context of the decision statement to fully understand the implications of the decision. Decision statements and decision context descriptions should always be considered in pairs. A decision statement might be to select a car for the governor of California. The context statement might be: The car shall demonstrate sensitivity to the environment and the willingness of the governor to set a green example by "walking the walk," or more appropriately, "driving the drive."

The Power of Framing

Framing is an effective technique used to differentiate the relevant from the irrelevant (see Figure 3.1). Pictures are framed to focus the observer on the content of the frame and to reduce the effect of

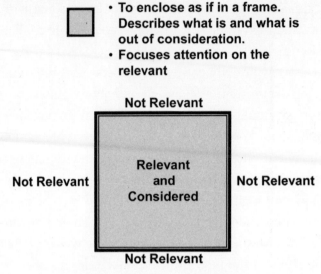

- To enclose as if in a frame. Describes what is and what is out of consideration.
- Focuses attention on the relevant

Figure 3.1   Framing Basics.

the surroundings that can be distractive to and in conflict with what is enclosed by the frame. Art galleries are experts in the framing of artwork to enhance the content to the exclusion of the surroundings.

To help think clearly about decisions there are two decision process frames that focus the process to the relevant. The first frame is the decision type frame that addresses the decision statement and context, what is at stake, and the potential impact of the possible outcomes. The second decision frame is the decision solution frame that represents the criteria that all candidate alternatives must satisfy to be considered and judged for acceptance.

The Decision Type Frame

When you witness people speaking of decisions they will typically describe or identify decisions as big, small, major, minor, urgent, difficult, snap, and similar words that are emotionally qualitative and not much help in clearly understanding what is at stake or the difficulty of the choice being faced.

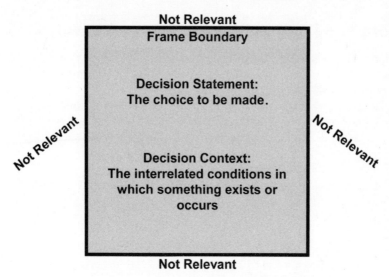

Figure 3.2   Decision Type Frame Core.

The decision type frame is structured to identify high stake decisions that if made badly can result in a highly negative outcome with serious consequences. Decisions that are determined to be high stake should be subjected to a rigorous decision process to ensure the best choice and action.

The Decision Type Frame encloses and responds to the decision statement and the context already developed earlier. There are four sides to the frame that characterize the type of decision being faced (see Figure 3.2).

Frame Side 1: Possible Bad Outcome

Decision type frame side number 1 addresses whether the decision can result in a very bad outcome such as a failed marriage, loss of employment, loss of wealth, loss of a client, and so forth. Decisions about food, movies, and music are relatively benign with not much at stake unless you are allergic to some foods or you are a candidate on *American Idol* and you make the wrong song choice, which could

Cord Too Long in Bungee Jump—Denver, CO

A man who was killed Sunday in a bungee jump was attached to a cord that was 70 feet too long, an industry investigator said today.

Mr. xxxx, 20, was taking a free jump in exchange for testing the equipment when he leaped from a tethered hot-air balloon over a field. The police are considering homicide charges against officials of the Denver-based company.

Mr. yyyy's report, which was turned over to the police, concluded that the balloon had been hovering at 190 feet when the length of the cord required it to hover at 260 feet.

Figure 3.3   Possible Bad Outcome.

Source: Excerpted and paraphrased from *New York Times*, July 2, 1993.

be a career-limiting decision. While we make many low-stake decisions without serious incidence, there are routine decisions like jaywalking that don't seem serious but have the potential of resulting in a very bad outcome. Jaywalking, like bungee jumping and skydiving, has a lot at stake. All three can result in death if not carefully managed (see Figures 3.3 and 3.4).

Two Skydivers Fall to Their Deaths—Los Angeles, CA

PJM, a sky diving instructor who had made more than 17,000 jumps and CDS died Thursday when their parachutes collided and deflated and they plunged to the ground.

The U.S. Parachute Association recorded 21 fatal skydiving accidents in the United States last year, down from an average of nearly 26 annual deaths from 2000 to 2009.

Figure 3.4   Possible Bad Outcome.

Source: Excerpted and paraphrased from *Daily Mail Reporter*, April 1, 2011.

Frame Side 2: Possible Permanent Outcome

Decision type frame side number 2 addresses whether the decision outcome is permanent and nonchangeable. Permanent decisions cause permanent consequences (outcomes) that will be either permanently positive outcomes (successes) or permanently negative outcomes (also called permanent errors). Once the decision action occurs the consequence cannot be altered. The sending of an e-mail is permanent, as the e-mail cannot be retrieved. Conversely, the consequences of nonpermanent decisions can be altered after the fact just as a bad meal can be exchanged for a different selection.

Examples of successful permanent decisions are earning of a college degree, successful organ transplant, successful missile launch, and successful auction bid. Skydiving and bungee jumping are vivid examples of permanent decisions that can have either a good or bad outcome.

Two startling examples of permanent errors are friendly fire casualties (known as fratricide) and wrong-site surgery, where planned surgery is administered to the wrong patient or to the incorrect part of a patient. The act of firing any weapon is a permanent decision, as you cannot reel the projectile back in, and if the weapon is not pointed correctly can result in a permanent error. The U.S. Marines reports 23 friendly fire incidents from 2001 to 2007, causing 82 casualties. The U.S. Army reports 24 friendly fire casualties in Iraq and 35 in Desert Storm.

The permanent errors of wrong-site surgery and incorrect administering of medication continue to plague our health-care system. The Archives of Surgery, August 2007 reports that there are 1,300 to 2,700 wrong-site surgeries performed each year.[1] This is a stunning statistic, given that preventing many of the wrong-site surgeries only takes a felt pen and a simple, very effective process called "cut through the ink." When I was being prepared for rotator cuff surgery, three different nurses each had me mark the location of my surgery with a felt pen of a unique color. My three personal

---

[1]www.archsurg.com.

markings and the surgeon's commitment to cut through the marks was our binding agreement for this permanent surgery decision. Recent wrong-sited surgeries have included mistakes with amputations and brain surgery, incorrect organ removal, and surgery on the wrong patient (see Figure 3.5). The simple "cut through the ink" process could have prevented these errors.

On August 10, 2009, the *San Francisco Chronicle* reported in a feature story titled, "Dead by Mistake" that 98,000 people per year die in the United States from preventable medical errors. Each fatal error is caused by a medical practitioner making a flawed decision with the potential of a bad permanent outcome.

Other permanent errors can be loss of reputation, earning a police record, dishonorable discharge, and first illegal drug use. These consequences are permanent for life, and like all permanent errors, while you can apologize for them, you cannot change them. It is important to understand that all first-time decisions are permanent decisions and may narrow life's opportunities. For example, a single first-time illegal drug use forever prevents a person from legitimately claiming no illegal drug use on employment applications without falsifying the application. This considerably reduces employment opportunities.

The permanency of our decisions is rapidly increasing as security and personal video cameras unknowingly capture our actions (sometimes to our embarrassment). While this seems to be an invasion of privacy, the

Botched Transplant
Posted – Feb 18, 2011

SAN FRANCISCO, California—USC University Hospital shut down its kidney transplant program last month after a kidney was accidentally transplanted to the wrong patient, according to a spokesman for the program that coordinates transplants.

Figure 3.5   Possible Bad Outcome.

Source: Excerpted and paraphrased from ABC News, February 18, 2011.

positive side is that these same cameras often provide needed evidence in criminal cases. They also can provide evidence of out-of-courtroom behavior that can reveal a defendant's true state of mind.

In Providence, Rhode Island, a 20-year-old student seriously injured a woman while he was driving drunk. While the woman was in the hospital recuperating the accused man was videoed impersonating a prisoner while drinking at a Halloween party, thereby mocking his felonious behavior. It was broadcast on Facebook and got into the hands of the prosecuting attorney who presented it to the judge as evidence of an "unrepentant defendant" who partied while his victim tried to recover in the hospital. The judge agreed, called the pictures depraved, and sentenced the man to prison.

More recently, a Canadian woman on work disability for severe depression was videoed being quite active at Chippendale's, ogling men in an all-male revue. Her videos were posted on Facebook and were discovered by her employer, who promptly terminated her disability payments. Another example of the power of digital permanence.

"Social networking sites are just another way that people say things or do things that come back to haunt them," says Phil Malone, director of the Cyberlaw Clinic at Harvard Law School. "The things that people say online or leave online are pretty permanent." Unauthorized personal photographs and videos have been placed on the Web by third parties, to the significant embarrassment of the affected person. Unfortunately, having them removed is virtually impossible, as they are copied and distributed almost instantly.

Congressional Representative Anthony D. Weiner found this to be too true as his sexy Facebook communications were widely distributed to the press and beyond (see Figure 3.6). While his actions were not illegal, the embarrassment to his coworkers and the government in general was so significant that he resigned under pressure from members of his own party on Capitol Hill. The ultimate outcome of his decision was the election of a Republican to the seat he held, which for Weiner is a very undesirable outcome. His now tarnished reputation is likely to shadow him for some time to come.

Congressman Weiner Admits to Internet Affairs
June 6, 2011
Rep. Anthony Weiner, D-N.Y., apologizes for photos sent to women on Twitter.
Rep. Anthony Weiner said today he has engaged in "several inappropriate" electronic relationships with six women over three years, and that he publicly lied about a photo of himself sent over Twitter to a college student in Seattle over a week ago.
"I take full responsibility for my actions," Weiner said. "The picture was of me, and I sent it."

Figure 3.6   Permanent Outcome.

Source: Excerpted and paraphrased from ABC News, June 6, 2011.

Michael Phelps, winner of eight gold medals at the 2008 Olympics, made a bad decision as evidenced by pictures of his marijuana smoking that appeared on the Internet, where they are indelibly permanent. This single act caused Phelps to be suspended from competing for three months and also caused Phelps to lose millions in lucrative corporate sponsorships as sponsors distanced themselves from his bad decision making. Kellogg, a major sponsor, did not renew his product endorsement and has proclaimed that Phelps's behavior "is not consistent with the image of Kellogg." The image that Phelps's actions portrayed was so offensive to Kellogg that they recalled all of their products that included Phelps's picture and donated the food to charity. Consistent with permanent error decision behavior, Phelps has apologized for his action, but the damage is permanent and irrevocable and his reputation has been permanently stained (see Figure 3.7).

Squeaky clean Tiger Woods, with the most wholesome image in professional sports, admitted to multiple affairs. His decision to participate in these relationships compromised his marriage, his family, his career, and his many sponsor relationships (see Figure 3.8). This is another vivid example of a permanent error. As is typical with

> # I'm sorry, says Michael Phelps
> Olympic hero Phelps issues apology over dope pipe photo
>
> *"I am sorry. I promise my fans and the public it will not happen again."*
>
> *"I engaged in behavior which was regrettable and demonstrated bad judgment,"* Phelps said.

Figure 3.7   Permanent Outcome.

Source: Excerpted and paraphrased from NBC News, February 2, 2009.

permanent errors, Tiger Woods has apologized but the damage cannot be erased or corrected and his reputation will be forever tarnished.

There are also near-permanent decisions where undesirable consequences can be corrected, but often the effort, risk, and cost is prohibitive or almost prohibitive. The Hubble Space Telescope is a famous example. The original decision to launch the Hubble into orbit was based on flawed verification data. The Hubble was successfully placed into orbit but with a defective mirror that produced unusable blurred images. At first, the consequences appeared to be a permanent outcome. But engineers conceived a way of adding a corrective lens that required another shuttle launch and very

> # Tiger apologizes, unsure when he'll return to golf
>
> **PONTE VEDRA BEACH, Fla. (AP)**
> Tiger Woods apologized Friday for cheating on his wife and says he is unsure when he will return to competitive golf.
>
> *"I was unfaithful. I had affairs. I cheated. What I did was not acceptable,"* said Woods, looking composed and speaking in a steady voice. His wife, Elin, was not with him.
>
> **Tiger's reputation is permanently damaged. His marriage, not permanent, has ended.**

Figure 3.8   Permanent Outcome.

Source: Excerpted and paraphrased from WSJ News, February 20, 2010.

high-risk space walks by the astronauts to install it. This was a very expensive and risky correction of a decision's bad outcome.

Frame Side 3: Uncertain Information

Frame side number 3 addresses whether the decision judgment must be based on uncertain information as opposed to factual data. Most of life's decisions can be based on factual data if we are diligent enough to seek it out. The Internet, with its prolific search engines, has made information resources conveniently available. Unfortunately, many decision makers don't bother to research and proceed to make decisions that are not supported by facts. Decisions that must be made based on uncertainty are the most difficult and are treated in detail in Chapter 8. Medical decisions where the symptoms are not understood are in this category. Business decisions that must be made without knowing what the competition is planning are also in this category.

Frame Side 4: Binding Agreement

Decision type frame side number 4 addresses whether the decision results in a binding agreement on others. With the exception of binding contracts, in our culture we are often unclear as to when we are party to a binding agreement.

Binding means an imposing or commanding adherence to a commitment, an obligation, or a duty. A binding decision is one where all parties agree to be bound to the decision action. Agreement changes are permissible but binding agreements require coordination and agreement between the parties regarding any change. This distinction is important to the quality of interpersonal relationships and the practice of "make a promise, keep a promise" credibility. Nonbinding agreements involve the decision maker alone and a change in action is at the decision maker's discretion since there is no required change coordination.

We tend to be too casual about our binding agreements. When I invite guests to dinner and they agree to arrive at 6:00 PM, I believe that I have a binding agreement with them and any change should trigger discussions relative to a new arrival time. If my guests arrive late with no advanced coordination, it is evidence that they did not share this binding concept or the practice of change coordination. This lack of coordination may result in an overdone dinner and cause relationship tensions to develop.

The concept of binding decisions is important to family harmony. If a parent says to a teen "I want you to clean your room," and the teen says, "Okay," is that a binding decision or not? To ensure that it is, a friend of mine has his teen look him in the eyes when committing to do something. That simple gesture works in his case and he gets the binding agreement and decision action that he is seeking.

Spousal harmony is often compromised by the lack of clarity in binding agreements. One may seek help from the other and get what appears to be a decision and agreement to provide the help, only to be ignored later. This practice of not honoring "binding agreements" can lead to disappointment, conflict, and separating emotions.

Binding agreements are especially important to business success. One needs to know when they can count on an agreement and when it is likely to be just lip service and subsequently ignored. The custom of "Let's shake on that" has been a long accepted gesture signifying a binding agreement. Figure 3.9 shows several gesture indicators of entering into a binding agreement.

We need to make visibly apparent the nature of our agreements. Too often we operate based on unstated assumptions that are incorrect. Sometimes we only pay cursory attention to a discussion that is headed toward a binding decision and we overlook the seriousness of the binding outcome. As a result we proceed to the decision without properly considering the relevant facts that were discussed and not heard or should have been discussed and were not because of our lack of attention. Discussions that are a preamble to a desired binding decision should be declared as such at the outset to alert all participants of the seriousness of the content. Then when the

Figure 3.9   Binding Agreement Gestures.

decision has been made it should be confirmed by all affected. Several U.S. government agencies have adopted the policy of issuing a Record of Decision, known as an ROD, as the evidence of a binding decision.

If one chooses to ignore their binding agreements and routinely breaks promises it will permanently damage their reputation. Damaged reputations are very difficult to repair and are usually not repairable to the predamaged state.

The following news article in Figure 3.10 is an example of not honoring a binding agreement. In this case it may be that only one of the handshake parties viewed the decision as binding.

Individuals and organizations need to introduce clarity into the management of binding decisions. Some organizations work to an approved baseline that contains the binding decisions that must be respected by all. Any change to the baseline decisions requires approval by a change management system, sometimes called a change board, which ensures proper coordination among

Mayor Accused of Breaking Handshake on Transit—San Francisco, CA

San Francisco Mayor Gavin Newsom broke a promise to withdraw a measure from the November ballot that would change the makeup of the panel that oversees the city's transit system, a steaming-mad city supervisor charged on Friday.

"The mayor is the most duplicitous elected official in the city of San Francisco," a fuming McGoldrick said Friday evening. "His word is not worth the breath it takes for him to expel it. He's a total phony who's fooled a lot of people for too long."

McGoldrick and Newsom never had any such deal, said Nathan Ballard, the mayor's press secretary.

Figure 3.10   Breaking a Promise.

Source: Excerpted and paraphrased from *SF Chronicle*, August 2, 2008.

the affected stakeholders of the decision. Less formal environments may adopt the gesture of a handshake or dual thumbs up to indicate a binding agreement. Many have adopted a practice of orally verbalizing, "So we have a binding agreement?" to confirm that there is one.

A developer I know has started applying this same technique with his contractors, especially when discussing cost and schedule promises.

In many business environments binding agreements are posted for all to see, especially when they involve organizational rules of behavior and safety issues.

Intel Corporation, the world's largest semiconductor manufacturer, developed a culture of make a promise, keep a promise binding decisions. To foster the culture team members were encouraged (obligated) to hold each other accountable to their agreements using constructive confrontation. As a comparison of cultures I provided consulting for a U.S. government agency in the United Kingdom. The subject project was in deep trouble and it did not take long to discover that hardly anyone delivered on their promises, and excuses for delay were accepted without any consequences. There was a cavalier treatment of commitments to where no one expected them to be met. This example is in sharp contrast to the Intel culture and to my aerospace culture experience, where customer commitments were considered sacred and mandatory to be met. In this U.K. project it was normal and acceptable within the culture to make and then ignore promises.

In both the *Challenger* and *Columbia* tragedies there were permanent decisions of very high significance made without the binding agreement that should have included those who would be affected the most, the flight crew. In both cases, the flight crews knew nothing of the technical concerns of the experts on the ground.

If the *Challenger* launch and the *Columbia* reentry decisions had been treated as permanent, binding decisions requiring the participation of the flight crews, it is highly probable the alternative selected would have been significantly different.

As a personal exercise relative to binding decisions, first estimate how many individuals you personally know in the world. These friends and acquaintances include personal, business, organizations, sports, neighbors, and so forth. The number will probably be in the hundreds and maybe even to the thousands. Write the number down. Now list the names of those individuals who you can reliably count on to deliver to their promises without question. For most people the number will fit within the number of fingers on two hands. It is a sad but true commentary on those who overpromise and underdeliver.

Decisions and Delegated Authority

A colleague shared the following experience after accepting a position with a new manager. Eager to be successful, he asked his manager what would determine how well he was doing in his new position with his new responsibilities. His manager provided this thoughtful answer.

There are decisions you will make that I don't need to know about.

There are decisions you will make that I need to be informed about.

And there are decisions you will want to make that I need to be involved in.

I will judge you by how well you know the difference in these three.

The Decision Type Frame

The decision type frame is based on the simple illustrated checklist in Figure 3.11.

The resultant decision type frame, based on this simple checklist, characterizes the type of decision and appears as follows in Figure 3.12.

The highest stake and most difficult decision appears as in Figure 3.13.

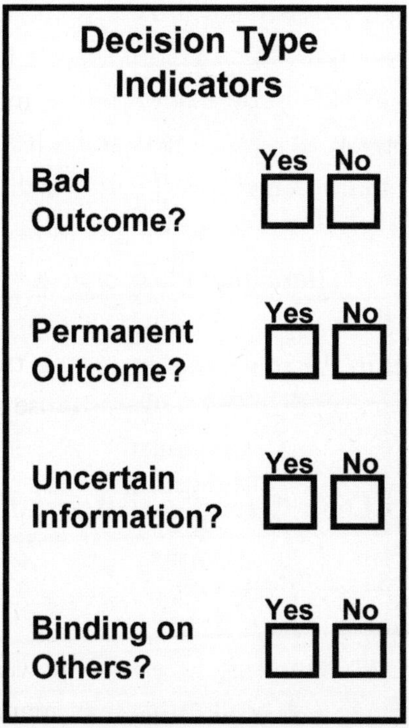

Figure 3.11   Decision Type Indicators.

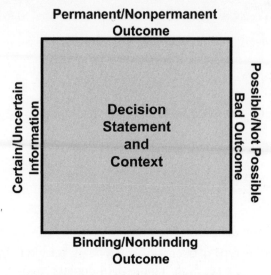

Figure 3.12 Decision Type Frame.

An example of this illustrated difficult decision type is whether to proceed with first-time experimental surgery for a serious illness. A second example occurs in time of warfare when there is potential targeting confusion on the battlefield and whether to fire or not. A firing decision may or may not be binding depending on the

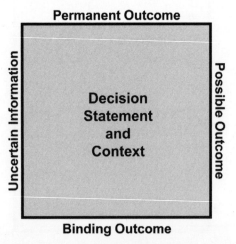

Figure 3.13 Most Difficult Decision.

targeting procedure. Risky situations often require independent target authentication from a targeting authority.

Assessing Decision Outcome Impact

The Impact of the Outcome

Decision impact and its significance is a personal assessment that involves both risk tolerance and the potential negative consequences. People with substantial assets can invest in the stock market and accept the associated risk. Those with minimum assets cannot afford the luxury of adopting those same risks. Decision significance is a measure of the personal tolerance for the potential negative outcomes combined with the permanency of the result. Figure 3.14 depicts this combination.

The same illustration, with examples, is shown in Figure 3.15.

By combining the decision impact just evaluated with the potential for information uncertainty we can evaluate the difficulty of making a judgment (see Figure 3.16).

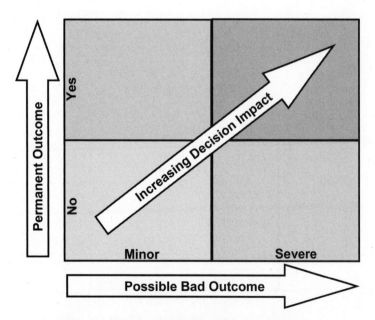

Figure 3.14 Decision Impact Matrix.

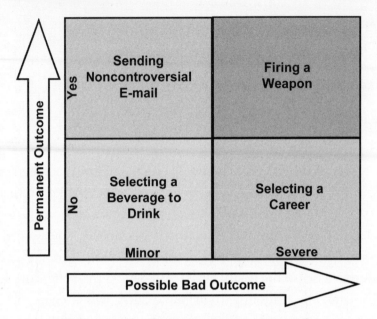

Figure 3.15 Decision Impact Example.

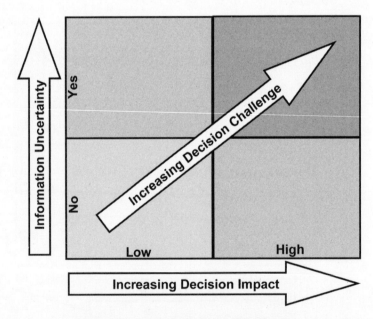

Figure 3.16 Decision Challenge.

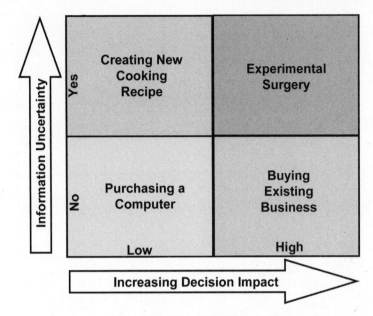

Figure 3.17   Decision Challenge Example.

The illustration, with examples, is shown in Figure 3.17.

Experimental surgery combines both the high impact of a possible bad outcome that can be permanent with the circumstance of dealing with no prior history or facts to extrapolate from. Decisions of this kind are challenging even for the most experienced decision maker and it comes down to the amount of confidence in the person carrying out the decision action.

By combining the aspect of binding agreements with information uncertainty we can address the difficulty in achieving consensus. If consensus is required among stakeholders and the judgment must be made on uncertain information, then consensus will be a challenge to achieve.

Figure 3.18 provides the associated model.

Figure 3.19 shows the model with examples.

An interesting perspective is to map examples of decisions in the permanent/binding combinations. The following provides examples for consideration. See if you can accurately add at least one to each category.

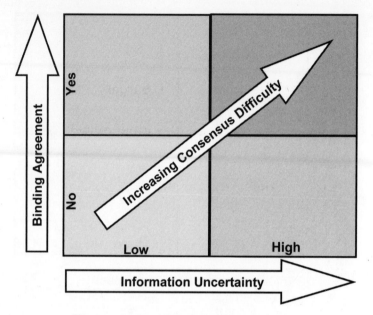

Figure 3.18   Decision Consensus.

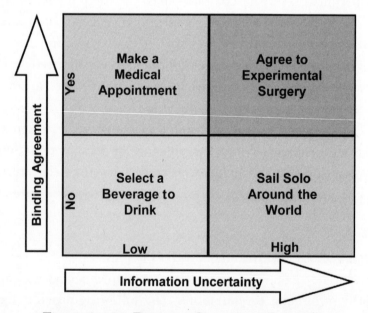

Figure 3.19   Decision Consensus Example.

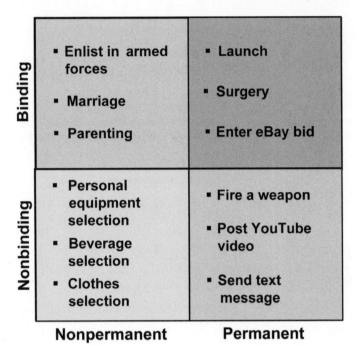

Figure 3.20   Permanent/Binding Examples.

This matrix in Figure 3.20 reveals four quadrants of dual conditions.

In the nonpermanent nonbinding quadrant there are three selections that can be done independently and can be changed at will by the decision maker without further coordination.

The binding nonpermanent quadrant contains three decisions that, while very outcome significant, do not have permanent outcomes. There are ways of leaving the armed forces, including going AWOL, which is a permanent error. Marriages can be annulled and can also be ended by divorce. Parenting appears permanent but children can be put up for adoption and in Los Angeles newborn children can be dropped off at local fire stations with no questions asked. The binding part of raising children is not between the parent and the child since the child is too young to make a binding agreement. Rather, it is between the parent and the state that makes it illegal for the parent to abandon children without the state's agreement.

Law Allows Abandonment of Teens
OMAHA, Neb.

Nebraska regulation lets parents drop off miscreant or disabled kids.

Nebraska's new "safe-haven" law allowing parents to abandon unwanted children at hospitals with no questions asked is unique in a significant way: It goes beyond babies and potentially permits the abandonment of anyone under 19.

Figure 3.21   Nonpermanent Parenting.
Source: Excerpted and paraphrased from *USA Today*, August 22, 2008.

However, in some states there is now a binding agreement that the parent can abandon their child with the state's approval. The news article in Figure 3.21 describes Nebraska's regulation (doctrine) that permits parents to abandon their children under certain circumstances.

This provision has already had some takers, as the following two news articles in Figures 3.22 and 3.23 explain. These are unintended consequences of this decision doctrine, which was directed to helping infants in trouble.

The permanent nonbinding quadrant contains three very personal decisions that once acted upon led to permanent and irreversible outcomes. It is noteworthy that sending a text message is permanent and parenting your children is not.

The final binding and permanent quadrant contains three examples. Any launch decision requires the binding agreement of

First Two Older Youths Left at Nebraska Havens
OMAHA, Neb.

Two boys ages 15 and 11 were left at Nebraska hospitals over the weekend, the first youngsters surrendered under the state's new safe haven law that allows caregivers to abandon children and teens as well as infants, officials said.

Figure 3.22   Unintended Consequences.
Source: Excerpted and paraphrased from *USA Today*, September 26, 2008.

Nine Kids in Family Abandoned at Omaha Hospital
OMAHA, Neb.

Nine siblings are among 11 children as old as 17 who were left at Omaha hospitals Wednesday under Nebraska's unique and new safe haven law, which allows caregivers to abandon babies and teenagers alike to hospitals without fear of prosecution.

Figure 3.23   More Unintended Consequences.

Source: Excerpted and paraphrased from MSNBC, September 26, 2008.

all stakeholders involved. Surgery requires the binding agreement between the patient and the doctor and possibly the obligated insurance company as well. All eBay auction bids are binding agreements per the terms of the website and the auction outcome is permanent.

Another example of a permanent and binding decision is the *Atlantis* shuttle reentry decision of August 2007. It was a successful binding/permanent decision made by both the flight crew and ground-based experts to land without repairing the known defects in the protective insulation. If the decision had been incorrect the *Atlantis* could have been destroyed like *Columbia*. Permanent decisions require the extra care necessary to make sure they result in the best possible choice as the outcomes cannot be altered once the action has been initiated.

There are permanent decisions that must be made in an instant such as the quarterback's pass in football and the batter's decision to swing at a pitch. Both of these may be binding or nonbinding decisions depending on the tactics employed and the signals communicated by other team members at the time.

Law enforcement personnel are often faced with the need to make an instantaneous nonbinding permanent decision of whether to fire their weapon at a threatening suspect that could maim or kill. The decision is nonbinding since to consult with a superior for permission would take too long and the officer would lose the opportunity of the moment. Unfortunately, some officers of the law react too hastily when firing their weapon only to kill unarmed or innocent suspects. It is not unusual for them to be charged with a crime and sometimes lose their profession.

The submission of a proposal in response to a request for proposal (RFP) or a bid in response to an invitation to bid (ITB) are both permanent decisions that once made are irrevocable, much the same as an auction bid made at a public auction. If you lose you have lost and if you win you have won. The only alternative is to formally protest the award based on improper buyer conduct, which is not likely to prevail.

Revisiting the decision type frame it becomes apparent that the combination of a potential bad outcome and outcome permanency drives the decision rigor so as not to make a serious error in judgment (see Figure 3.24). The uncertainty in the information drives the extent of investigation and analysis to reduce the critical uncertainties. If the decision is to result in a binding agreement, this will drive the effort to communicate, coordinate, and collaborate toward achieving stakeholder consensus.

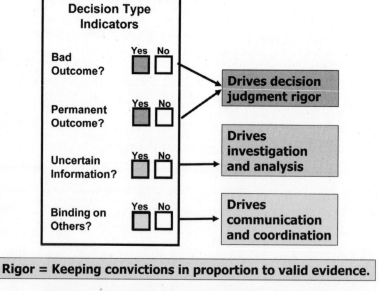

Figure 3.24   Decision Type Frame Impact.

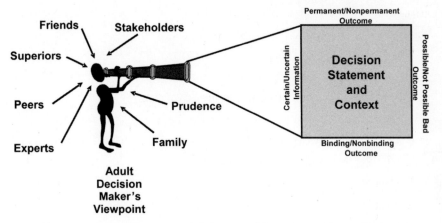

Figure 3.25   Decision Maker and Decision Type Frame.

The Decision Maker and the Decision Type Frame

The decision maker's view of a decision is shaped by many factors, including the inputs of valued stakeholders. The decision maker has the challenge of blending these inputs into a meaningful decision statement, a proper context, and the decision type frame that characterizes the decision and communicates to others what is at stake and what the challenges are.

Figure 3.25 depicts this challenge.

A decision-fit decision maker should be sufficiently skilled to handle this challenge.

The Bases for Judgment

Decision Action

All decisions require the selection of an action from two or more suitable alternatives. Decisions in the "should I?" and "shouldn't I?" categories only require the selection of one of a pair of alternatives. Within this category are many quality of life decisions such as education, marriage, profession, location, religion, and so forth.

Business decisions involve both strategic and tactical decisions that can make or break business success. Business decisions often require the selection of an action from a group of viable alternatives.

There are at least 10 bases for the judgment of alternatives that are commonly applied. Often the wrong basis is used, which can lead to a less than optimum selection. In fact, it seems that there are more errors made in the selection of the basis of judgment than there are in the flawed application of judgment processes. *Most decision errors stem from allowing emotion and intuition to cloud what the evidence and facts reveal if they are properly considered.*

Instinct-Based Judgment

There is a debate as to whether humans react based on instinct as animals do. Proponents cite breathing, sex drive, crying, and the like as examples of actions caused by instincts. Fortunately, both sides agree that instinct-based actions are biological reactions that are not made by conscious and learned choice. This decision book is about humans deliberately judging and choosing and since instinct-based actions are not conscious choices but genetic predispositions they are not relevant to overt judging. When humans declare that they made a judgment by instinct they usually would be more accurate to claim they made the judgment by intuition.

Decision Judgment Model

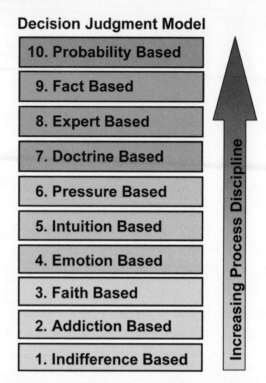

Figure 4.1   Decision Judgment Model.

Decision Judgment Bases

Ten prevalent judgment bases are shown in Figure 4.1.

You have probably witnessed people making decisions based on many of these judgments. But you have probably never seen all 10 clustered and ranked. This is a first. While not an exact science, these bases are sequenced from bottom to top to represent the increasing processes rigor required to properly judge and choose wisely. This will be covered in detail.

1. Indifference-Based Judgment

This is judgment and selection of an alternative by chance or delegation. It is sometimes termed the "whatever" judgment method where a person overtly defers to others such as in the selection of a restaurant or a wine or where we simply fail to act on a required action. Methods of selection in this category can include flipping a coin, drawing straws, or choosing to accept the default selection made for us by a choice architect. Care should be exercised when selecting the indifference mode to ensure that you are really indifferent. For instance, if you proclaim your indifference in selecting a restaurant for dinner and then someone selects a restaurant you strongly dislike, you may quickly discover that you are not really indifferent. The key is to challenge and test your indifference before you proclaim it, or reserve veto power over another's selection.

Choice Architects are those that preconfigure default settings to make it simple and easy for us to accept their selections and go along with the architect's choices. Choice Architects can leverage this judgment basis by constructing default choices to benefit their own strategic objectives. Employers offer carefully selected defaults for savings and health plans and computer software companies and cell phone makers build in default configuration settings that can be overridden by overt user action. However, it is a measured fact that most users do not deviate from the default settings. Once employees select a savings or insurance plan they seldom alter it over the life of their employment, and most electronics users remain with their default settings.

It can be tactically useful to defer to others on decisions of low importance to you so that later when a judgment matters, you can weigh in stronger, having acquiesced earlier.

2. Addiction-Based Judgment

This is judgment and selection of an alternative based on the *uncontrollable* desire to satisfy a personal need. When people apply addiction-based judgment they typically turn a blind eye to contradictory evidence that does not support their actions. Common examples are abuse of tobacco, alcohol, drugs, gambling, and food. Our society is plagued with the community costs of addicts who continue to allow their addictive need to bias their decision judgment. Logic and expert opinion usually have little effect until the addict decides to change and takes personal responsibility and initiates the action to do so. Many addicts have good intentions to change but are unable to rise to the challenge of taking decisive action to conquer their addiction. In these cases forced intervention is sometimes applied.

While "addiction" conjures up the well-known addictions already identified, addictions also exist in the business world. People and organizations can be addicted to their way of doing things or to a solution they are familiar and comfortable with. There are two NASA examples that have been reported by those familiar with the circumstances. The first had to do with the design of the shuttle orbiter. It seems that all test results justified a lifting body configuration for the orbiter. The lifting body is a design that does not have wings and the necessary lift is generated by the overall envelope of the spacecraft. However, NASA was made up of aeronautical engineers and pilots that were very partial to having wings on their flying machines. In the end, those addicted to wings prevailed and the shuttle completed its mission with those unnecessary wings. It is interesting that Russia copied the very same design for their Buran spacecraft, which also sports the unnecessary wings but was never put into routine service after initial testing.

The second NASA example of addiction-based judgment was the decision whether the first shuttle flight should be manned or unmanned. Because shuttle flights are inherently a high-risk endeavor there were many who sought to have the first flight unmanned. However, there were others who thought that if the first flight was unmanned then all flights could be unmanned and the role of the fight crew could be significantly diminished. Again, the pilots prevailed and the first flight and all flights since have been manned. It is interesting that in sharp contrast Russia chose to fly their first Buran flight as unmanned and they did so successfully and they continue to routinely fly their space station supply ship *Progress* to the International Space Station three to four times per year completely unmanned and have achieved almost no public recognition for this amazing technological feat.

In both of these examples the addiction to prior beliefs was combined with high emotional drive, which enabled the emotion-backed preferences to prevail.

There are newsworthy reports of researchers adjusting research results to support their concept or theory rather than acknowledging nonconfirming evidence. This too is evidence of making addiction-based judgment. We are all susceptible to being so enamored with one particular solution that we refuse to consider other and perhaps more viable solutions. This is sometimes called paradigm paralysis, to characterize when we are blinded by our own paradigm and thereby exclude all others, no matter how viable. The ignoring of nonconfirming test results or other contradictory evidence are examples of force fitting data to support an addiction-based belief.

The power of addiction in lifestyle decisions is evidenced by the 75 percent of our prison population who are incarcerated due to substance abuse related crimes. "The addiction made me do it" is a common refrain.

3. Faith-Based Judgment

This is judgment and selection of an alternative based on firm belief in something for which there is no proof. This faith-based reference is not specific to a named faith such as Catholic or Protestant. It pertains to faith-based judgments common to all religions, faith-based healing, holistic medicine, feng shui, gambling, astrology, and other areas where "blind faith" is preferred over contradictory or no evidence. Courts have recently overruled parents' decisions to apply faith-based healing to their children when experts testify in court that without proven expert-based medical treatment the children are likely to die. In these cases the courts act in the best interests of the children based on scientific evidence.

An example of the power of faith-based commitment is the unfortunate death of three executives who were encouraged by a self-proclaimed guru to sweat it out in a too-hot tent in the middle of the desert (see Figure 4.2). When they wanted to leave he encouraged them to stick it out to become superior to others who had waffled. It is almost incomprehensible that intelligent and successful executives would elect to spend thousands of dollars to follow a self-proclaimed expert without appropriate credentials. James Ray has been found guilty of negligent homicide. While on trial he continued to sell self-help seminars and books.

Self-Help Guru Arrested on Murder Charges
Feb. 3, 2010

A self-help guru who organized an Arizona sweat lodge ceremony last year in which three people died was arrested on manslaughter charges, authorities said.
James Ray, renowned for his best-selling books on spirituality, was arrested Wednesday at a law office in Prescott, Arizona close to the Sedona retreat where the fatal October ceremony was held.

James Ray Found Guilty of Negligent Homicide in Sweat Lodge Case
June 22, 2011

Self-help guru James Ray has been convicted of negligent homicide in the deaths of three participants in an Arizona sweat lodge ceremony, but he was found not guilty of manslaughter charges.
Prosecutors claimed that Ray's recklessness in operating the sweat lodge caused the deaths. Event participants paid up to $10,000 to seek "new areas of consciousness" at the October 2009 Spiritual Warrior retreat in the desert, according to trial testimony.

Figure 4.2 Deadly Faith-Based Example.

Source: Excerpted and paraphrased from ABC NEWS, June 22, 2011.

4. Emotion-Based Judgment

This is judgment and selection of an alternative based on personal emotion and feelings rather than facts or other quantitative factors. This approach is sometimes called judgment from the heart. Emotion-based judgment is valuable and applicable in the selection of alternatives that have aesthetic characteristics like clothing and decorator items and also in judgments relative to situations of high emotional content such as weddings and funerals. Emotion-based judgment is usually not suitable for physics, science, and legal-based decisions. Many businesses get started and quickly fail when the proprietors become enamored with the concept of being in business without doing the homework and quantitative analysis that it takes to be successful.

Teenagers frequently choose wild hairstyles, body piercings, tattoos, and other identity declarations strictly by emotion, with no analysis of the immediate or long-term consequences of their decisions. Although there is an abundance of factual information on the Internet relative to these decisions, teenagers seldom seek it out or consider it in their judgment.

Dan Ariely, in his book, *Predictably Irrational*, provides the results of insightful experimentation that confirms humans alter their logic, honesty, and character according to their emotional state, which in turn alters their ability to apply good judgment. It is often difficult to keep emotions out of decisions that should be driven by fact-based logic.

This is particularly true with real estate brokers who encounter buyers who become emotionally attracted to a flawed property and refuse to acknowledge or consider the short- and long-term problems associated with the flaws in the property. It becomes a "don't confuse me with the facts" situation.

Dr. Laura Schesslinger, whose talk show had over 7 million daily listeners, did her best to motivate troubled callers to set their feelings (emotions) aside and instead consider the evidence-based facts of their situation and then to make their judgment based on those facts rather than how they feel. It is disturbing how many of the callers were unable to ignore their feelings and simply face the hard, cold facts. Major decisions such as marriage, divorce, adultery, and family estrangements are often based solely on feelings, while ignoring relevant facts that would signal decision caution.

Buyer's remorse is an emotional condition whereby a person feels regret after a purchase decision that is typically emotion based. It is frequently associated with the purchase of higher value items. In some circumstances, to provide for buyer's remorse, a buyer may have the legal right to cancel a contract within a specified "cooling-off period," typically three days in duration. This right to cancel a contract is governed by both state and federal law.

Extreme cases of emotion-based judgment can lead to anger, violence, road rage, murder, or suicide, where the perpetrator loses control and succumbs to the most extreme negative emotions being experienced. Defendants sometimes enter a plea of insanity when being prosecuted for their emotion-based illegal actions.

On the positive side, emotion-based judgment is very useful in making a final selection among close competing fact-based alternatives, all of which offer a similar satisfactory solution.

5. Intuition-Based Judgment

This is judgment and selection of an alternative based on immediate perceived understanding without reasoning or inferring. There is a wide range of interpretations of intuition and no common understanding. The perceptions range from pure guessing all the way to making decisions based on relevant informed judgment but falling short of expert-based analysis and judgment. One Internet definition claims that "Intuition is regarded as a conscious commonality between earthly knowledge and the higher spiritual knowledge and appears as flashes of illumination" (Lorenzo Ravagli, *Zanders Erzahlungen*).

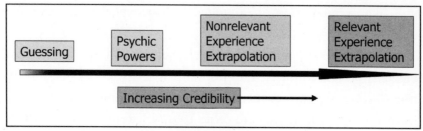

Intuition—A View

Figure 4.3   The Range of Intuition.

The model in Figure 4.3 depicts the range of common perceptions. Dilbert (Figure 4.4) understands the risk of applying intuition.

Intuition Comes in Many Forms

Some interpretations of intuition even include the influence of psychic powers, mental telepathy, and premonition. It is sometimes termed *snap judgment* and is commonly viewed as based on "gut reaction" and may be applied spontaneously in new situations requiring quick reaction such as accidents and disasters of various kinds.

Intuition is very valuable when applied by skilled emergency personnel in disaster situations when technicians are able to quickly extrapolate relevant past experiences to a current situation to arrive at an innovative and well-founded course of action. Intuition-based decisions that are successful typically result from a response that is rooted in relevant past experience. Intuition based on anything

Figure 4.4   Dilbert Gets It Right!

less, like extrapolation of nonrelevant past experience, can result in disaster.

Intuition can be appropriate when selecting a gift for a friend but can be risky and is inappropriate when the laws of physics rule in spite of contrary intuition. It is also inappropriate to apply intuition when facts are available that will render the intuition meaningless as demonstrated in Figure 4.5.

In Figure 4.5, quickly judge which line is longer.

Most people quickly judge line B to be longer than line A. Accurate measurement will reveal that just the opposite is true—a counterintuitive outcome.

There are many scientific and engineering situations that are counterintuitive. As you may recall from earlier descriptions in this book, the manager who made the decision not to seek photographs of the *Columbia* foam-impacted wing relied on her intuition that the foam couldn't damage the wing to the point that no attempt to ascertain the facts was made. It cost our nation seven astronauts' lives. Intuition can also be inappropriate when the significance of the decision is considered high, as in the following instance.

In July 2007, Homeland Security Secretary Chertoff raised the nation's al-Qaida threat level based on his "gut feel" (aka intuition). "What a jerk," said former FBI terror consultant Paul L. Williams

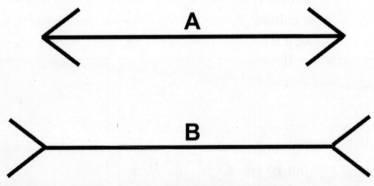

Figure 4.5   Intuition Exercise.

regarding Chertoff's intuition about terror attacks that summer. "The American people right now don't need the feeling of anybody. They need the sound judgment of officials." (From www.NewsMax.com, July 16, 2007.)

However, intuition can be very valuable when business visionaries conceive new products and new marketplaces before they exist and there is no available data to corroborate their decisions. The late Steve Jobs, Apple Corporation's founder and chairman, is an excellent example of this type of visionary. But for every Steve Jobs there are scores of others whose intuition-based predictions are never realized.

6. Pressure-Based Judgment—Power/Peer/Perk

This is judgment and selection of an alternative based on responding to the pressure of the power of authority, the pressure of peers, or the pressure of advantages (perks) that may be attached to certain decision alternatives. Time pressure is not relevant since time pressure influences when a judgment is made and may be a factor in decision fatigue but is not relevant to the basis of the judgment. Any of the 10 bases of judgment can be driven by the need for urgency but urgency is not a justification for using an inappropriate judgment basis.

Executive-based decisions help focus the enterprise on the organization's strategic objectives and that is desirable. It is good when the organization experiences the existence of an executive by the strength of the culture and the executive's influence on the culture. On the flip side, it is disturbing when an executive publicly overrules a specialist's well-formed decision. The term micro-management stems from managers who insist on overriding most of the decisions made by their expert staff.

Authority and peer pressure-based decisions (decisions to "go along") are often motivated by the fear of the consequences of not doing so. To not go along with the pressure from superiors could earn a reprimand or worse, and from peers it could result in hostility and exclusion from the peer group. In business there may be executive pressure to compromise on ethics or legality. It is not unusual for employees to seek alternative employment when challenged by ethically compromising circumstances.

Teens often face peer pressure to take up drugs, smoking, truancy, tattoos, and even pressure to join a gang. A college career counselor at a private high school reports that about 20 percent of her students select their college based on parental or peer pressure, with many of them becoming disappointed with their choice later on. College and career selections are serious decisions that deserve very careful consideration to avoid the associated potentially permanent consequences.

There is an unfortunate example of misapplied executive power pressure-based judgment during the British Petroleum oil spill. It was disclosed that a BP drilling technician told a CBS 60 *Minutes* reporter that "chunks of rubber from the gasket had broken loose weeks before, but a supervisor brushed off concerns."

Perk pressure-based judgment is widely used in sales and bonus programs to get desired results. It is the timeless "What gets measured gets done" rule and is quite effective. Unfortunately, perks are also used effectively by the criminal element to incentivize team members to conduct unlawful activity. An excellent positive example of perk pressure-based judgment is the 2007 Oakland Freeway Repair, where a $200,000 a day schedule incentive on a 50-day schedule motivated C.C. Myers and Company to complete the full repair in only 26 days and earn $5 million in incentive.

The sad but highly visible example of peer pressure-based judgment in a negative direction was when eight Mt. Everest hikers died when competing guided groups ignored their carefully planned descent trigger times and continued their ascent too late to return safely (see the book *Into Thin Air*). None of the teams wanted to quit the ascent while others forged ahead.

7. Doctrine-Based Judgment

This is judgment and selection of an alternative based on doctrine. In this case doctrine is defined as the body of principles in a branch of knowledge or system of beliefs. We live in a civilized society rooted in the laws (doctrine) that guide daily behavior that we can and do rely on. Traffic laws, criminal laws, and business laws all set the standards for our daily interactions with one another, which we violate at the risk of legal prosecution.

There is religious doctrine that we choose to live by that is not enforced by legal prosecution but is subject to church-levied consequences. The Holy Bible, the Book of Mormon, and the Koran are examples of religious doctrine that are interpreted by humans in myriad ways and can strongly influence the decisions of those who believe in a particular interpretation. Unfortunately, extreme interpretations of religious doctrine have led to international conflict on a grand scale as zealots combine doctrine-based judgment with extreme emotion-based actions leading to violent protests, suicide bombings, and wars.

There is also doctrine in educational and professional organizations that govern the rules of behavior expected from members. Members are often required to "sign up" to the standards and sometimes must actually sign a commitment to do so.

Families may choose to have family imposed and managed doctrine (house rules or code of conduct) governing the rules of behavior of family members. Parents hope that their carefully conceived doctrine will guide responsible decision making.

Sometimes decisions are made based on traditions that generations pass on to their descendants. These traditions permeate their customs, rules of behavior, work practices, ethics, and the like. Although not usually written in a document, they function the same as doctrine-based guidance and judgment.

Doctrine-based judgment is easy to justify, as very little analysis is needed to defend "following the rules" or what is customary.

However, history has shown that the excuses of the perpetrators of war crimes and crimes against humanity have often been "just following the rules."

The United States currently has about one million attorneys and is graduating 45,000 per year. The purpose of these lawyers is to resolve alleged violations of doctrine that an accusing party has an issue with and also to create new doctrine. We are becoming increasingly controlled by doctrine and lawyers.

8. Expert-Based Judgment

This is judgment and selection of an alternative based on expert opinion without involving our own personal quantitative analysis. Expert judgment is commonly applied where unique and specialized knowledge is not easy for a layman to access or comprehend. Common areas of application are medicine, complex equipment repair, and legal and financial issues. While experts may actually internalize their own fact-based and probability-based judgments, nonexperts normally do not get involved to that level of detail and accept the expert's recommendation without further interrogation or investigation.

Selecting the right "expert" may be more difficult than it first appears. It is relatively easy to find an expert physician or mechanic by asking friends for references and making reference checks. But there are areas where the apparent expert, in spite of an impressive list of certifications and qualifications, lacks critical local knowledge. I have personally witnessed home owners who hire professionally certified architects, soil engineers, and structural engineers who as a group produce flawed designs and structures because of lack of local knowledge. Instead, the neighbors of the property were the actual "experts," as they had the benefit of years of critical local knowledge not apparent or known to the new property owners or their hired out-of-town professionals. It is interesting that in these examples, the "professionals" made no effort to search out local knowledge and later when confronted with the "local facts" promptly took an arrogant stand and trivialized the information value even in the face of indisputable facts and their flawed designs. They probably believed that by the time the flaws were discovered they would be long gone.

When seeking expert opinion make sure the expert is truly an expert in the specific subject matter and also in the relevant application of that subject matter. There have been well-intentioned investors who have been duped by "professionals" in walnut offices complete with diplomas and certifications that were counterfeit. It pays to have a background check, which is not overly expensive.

The difference between a true expert and an intuitionist is that an expert "knows" and an intuitionist "thinks that they know."

9. Fact-Based Judgment

This is judgment and selection of an alternative based on quantitative factual information containing little uncertainty. This approach is sometimes called "from the head" and in professional debating is often named "deliberate reasoning." Science, engineering, law, physics, construction, agriculture, manufacturing, accounting, finance, and so forth, all apply this approach if possible. It usually involves logic, relevant data, analysis, and process and often results in a "trade study" to facilitate the fact-based judgment. Fact-based is sometimes known as the *Consumer Reports* approach since *Consumer Reports* routinely publishes comprehensive trade matrices for product comparisons that lead to ranked conclusions.

Search engines put immense amounts of factual data at our fingertips. It is frustrating to me that people will make life-determining decisions based on emotion and peer pressure rather than seek out factual information relative to those decisions. The Internet can provide facts about career paths, salary expectations, the impact of smoking, the impact of not having a college degree, and just about any other decision facing a person. Unfortunately, many decisions are made based on intuition and emotion because the decision maker does not search out available relevant information to support a fact-based choice. Getting teens to search out facts to support fact-based decisions is a cultural challenge.

In business, if facts don't support the popular opinion or the intuition of the decision maker they are sometimes ignored or adjusted to reach a preconceived outcome. A decision-fit decision maker should recognize this rationalization and seek to focus the team on the proper decision basis and the best process to be used to implement the basis.

10. Probability-Based Judgment

This is judgment and selection of an alternative based on probability assessment of the uncertainties within the decision logic and/or the consequences of the alternatives. Often there is past history that can provide credible probabilities and predictions of outcomes. This is especially true of predicting outcomes such as weather and expectations related to common surgical procedures. But there are often conditions related to medical decisions and business decisions where future expectations of the various alternatives are highly uncertain. If time and money are available, decision makers may pursue experimentation and analysis to reduce the uncertainty relative to alternative outcomes. Care must be exercised to not spend in excess of what the information is worth to the decision maker. Companies sometimes get carried away and spend multiple times what the sought after information is worth without realizing what they have committed to.

In my 20-plus years of aerospace systems engineering we intentionally did the experimentation and investigation necessary to reduce all uncertainties to near zero. By doing this and incorporating fault tolerant robust designs we achieved success rates in the very high 90 percent range even with new designs.

There are situations where experimentation cannot help determine future probabilities and probability assignments amount to little more than best guesses. Automobile companies must best guess the future impact of fuel prices, emission laws, and customer buying trends long before evidence is available to accurately influence their design and engineering tactics.

Which Judgment Process Is Most Suitable?

While each of these 10 judgment approaches will arrive at a selection there are those judgment methods that are "defensible" when challenged by experts and those that are not. This is particularly important with decisions that must be defended to higher authority. Figure 4.6 illustrates the influence of this distinction.

Defensible and Nondefensible Judgments

It is common in business to review the decisions of others. This occurs in our courts, in corporate management reviews, in government

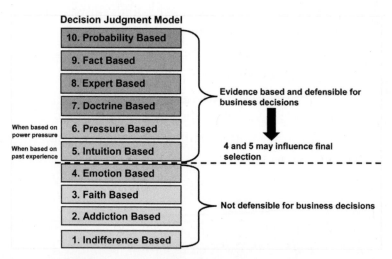

Figure 4.6   Defensible Judgment Bases.

oversight of projects, and in investor review of investment advisor tactics, among others. Some decision judgment bases are defensible and others would never pass the rigor of oversight scrutiny. The press frequently cites cases where the allure of personal gain has caused a businessman to stray from ethical practices to feather his own nest. A potential financial gain (perk) was incentive enough to cause straying over the line of ethical conduct.

Judgment bases numbered one through five on our list are difficult to defend as sound and logical except in the case of intuition when it is based on the proper extrapolation of relevant past experience to the current situation, which is the ideal application of intuition.

Pressure-based judgment is defensible when the pressure is from a person in authority who has jurisdiction over the issue at hand. However, if the decision action being requested is illegal, unsafe, or against the prevailing code of conduct, then it should be challenged and if possible recorded in some formal way. One should be wary of those who act like they have the authority but are not in fact vested with it. Responding to a counterfeit authority could be a career-limiting experience.

Pressure-based judgment that is perk based is defensible so long as the perks are legitimate, like sales campaign incentives. Illegal perks like kickbacks are not defensible to legal oversight.

Doctrine-based judgment is defensible when the doctrine is relevant, current, and not illegal or unsafe. The culture we live in is largely doctrine-based on the laws of the land, most of which we have never read but have heard about. Our culture is based on the acting out of the populace according to their perception of what the doctrine requires. Of course, there are portions of our society like the police who are watchful for violations egregious enough to require society to deliver corrective action.

Expert-based judgment is defensible if the expert has relevant and current expertise in the area requiring judgment. Expert witnesses in court cases usually must pass a vetting process to ensure the expert is truly an expert in the area under question. There are those who represent themselves as experts who have falsified their credentials and could not pass a vetting process. The certificates and plaques on their walls may be counterfeit. Hiring an independent to perform a background investigation could be money well spent.

Fact-based judgment is the most defensible of the judgment methods and there are various step-by-step processes to manage fact-based judgment. These will be detailed in subsequent chapters.

Probability-based judgment is defensible when the applied probabilities can be justified by experimentation, investigation, analysis, extrapolation, or some other method to establish the required credibility. If the applied probabilities are simply imaginary estimates without any foundation then the subsequent analysis will be suspect and cannot be defended.

As illustrated, emotion-based and intuition-based judgment are often combined with methods numbered 6 through 10 to settle on a final selection among alternatives judged to be near equally acceptable. For instance, in the case of selecting a vehicle to purchase, fact-based judgment will likely narrow the field of alternatives to a few almost equivalent candidates. Then test driving the finalists can introduce the emotional factor to influence the final judgment. This type of alternative judgment is credible and defensible and supports making judgments from both the head and the heart.

Combining methods does not always improve the judgment. The *Challenger* launch decision is famous for this. What had not been detected by other analysts is the following: The team started correctly using expert-based decision judgment to determine the launch readiness but the data was not presented in easily understood plots of O-ring charring versus temperature. Then when the O-ring seal experts could not prove a safe launch condition the executives started pursuing a "you haven't proven that it will fail" approach and pushed for additional facts relative to O-ring failures to determine launch readiness. Then when it was discovered that there were no additional relevant facts, the management shifted to referencing the documented booster specifications particular to launch readiness. The specifications (doctrine) provided for permissible launch from 40 degrees Fahrenheit to 90 degrees Fahrenheit, even though that capability had never been proven by qualification testing. With the predicted launch morning temperatures to be 28 degrees Fahrenheit these specifications (doctrine) would have to be violated. When the engineers still refused to confirm a safe launch, executives then applied their unfounded intuition and overrode both their own O-ring seal experts and their own booster design and launch specifications. Then to keep the engineers silent they applied the power of executive pressure so that when the booster team was asked if anyone had a different opinion from launching no one spoke up. (If the booster team members had been polled to individually state their name and their launch decision the results would have been different.) So the launch judgment basis progressed, or rather regressed, from expert-based, to fact-based, to doctrine-based, to intuition-based, to executive pressure–based to finally arrive at the outcome they wanted, which produced a bad decision and a bad outcome. The O-ring seals had never been tested for the prevailing cold temperature (which was in violation of the booster manufacturer's contract), and the O-ring seal failed due to being too stiff to seal at low temperatures. The rocket exhaust bypassed the O-ring seal, causing massive seal erosion and ultimate puncture of the fuel tank, and the *Challenger* exploded. It should be noted here that for this same *Challenger* launch many other doctrine-required no-go limits were also violated and waived by NASA management, any of which, if respected, would have held the flight. In the case of the *Challenger* launch decision, any decision-fit team member should have alerted the decision team of their flawed progression from expert-based action to executive pressure-based action, but none recognized they were traveling down that slippery slope to the final flawed decision judgment.

It is sad that the *Challenger* flight crew was not made aware of the dispute over launch readiness since at that time the flight crew was not part of the launch decision discussions concerning booster and ground support issues. Since any launch decision is a permanent decision with the potential of highly significant negative outcomes it should always be a binding decision with all affected parties reaching agreement. As a result of the *Challenger* accident, both flight and ground crews are now required to agree on the binding decision to launch.

Similarly, a Silicon Valley executive, piloting her own jet with her son aboard, was preparing to take off into a snowstorm and was advised by the tower (the experts) to de-ice. To their surprise she declined (using intuition?) and crashed shortly after takeoff, killing herself and her 10-year-old son. Her decision judgment went from expert-based (the controllers with local knowledge) to intuition-based, yielding a bad decision and a bad outcome. Had she treated her takeoff as a decision of high significance (possible permanent bad outcome) requiring a binding agreement between her and the flight controllers, she just may have averted the catastrophe. The controllers could not understand her reluctance to de-ice in the face of their informed recommendation.

A *USA Today* article describes the plight of multiple airline start-ups that are based on 100 percent business class where all have failed, and yet more are trying. The author states, "Nobody learns from previous mistakes. The rich businessmen only heed market research that agrees with their hunch (intuition) and ignore research (facts) that shows there aren't enough business class passengers to regularly fill their planes." (*USA Today*, June 5, 2008.) This is another example of what should be fact-based judgment yielding to intuition based in order to ignore contradictory evidence.

There are situations where intuition is extremely valuable and can trigger fact-based investigation to confirm or deny the intuition-based suppositions. Jaycee Dugard was kidnapped at age eleven and was held captive for eighteen years during which she was sexually abused and subsequently gave birth to two daughters fathered by her captor, Phillip Garrido. When Garrido showed up on the University of California campus with his two daughters to pass out religious leaflets a female security guard became suspicious of the behavior of both Garrido and the two emotionless girls. The intuition-based suspicion prompted a background check that confirmed Garrido was a paroled sex offender and further checking with his parole officer confirmed he had no children. He was arrested and is now serving a life sentence. In this case the combination of being a security guard and also being a mother and understanding normal daughter behavior prompted the well-founded suspicion of Garrido's situation. This is a sound example of intuition that is based on extrapolation of relevant past experience and knowledge to current evidence (see Figure 4.7).

Figure 4.8 reveals some common combined decision bases for selected examples.

Care must be exercised to match the judgment method to the significance of the decision. If the decision is considered trivial, such as what socks to wear, any method will suffice. However, if the decision is life-defining, with potential permanent consequences, then the most appropriate method should be adopted and the selection confirmed by including multiple expert judgments. In preparing a satellite for launch, our company would routinely have a technically competent independent team assess launch readiness in parallel with the responsible operating team. It required two coincidental "go"

Following a Hunch, Solving a Mystery
How intuition worked to free Jaycee Dugard

The FBI spent 18 years to find Jaycee Dugard, a girl abducted in 1991, when she was 11, while walking to her bus stop in South Lake Tahoe, CA. But when the case broke last week, it wasn't a sweeping raid or a well placed tip that eventually led the FBI to Dugard and the arrest of her captor, Phillip Garrido. It was intuition.

Figure 4.7 Intuition Properly Applied.

Source: Excerpted and paraphrased from *Newsweek*, August 31, 2009.

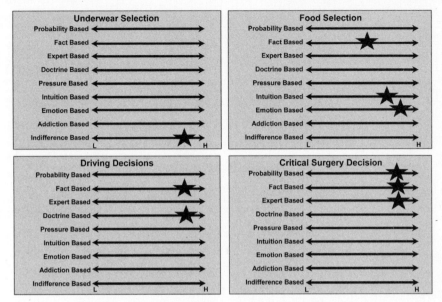

Figure 4.8   Examples of Typical Judgments.

decisions to authorize a highly significant, binding, and permanent launch decision.

Trust but Verify

Charles Ponzi is famous for developing an investment fraud that paid returns to investors out of the money paid by subsequent investors rather than from investment gains. The Ponzi scheme usually offers abnormally high short-term returns in order to entice new investors. The perpetuation of the advertised high returns requires an ever-increasing flow of new money from new and old investors in order to keep the scheme going.

Satisfied investors encourage even more new investors who in turn feed new money into the coffers to feed both the scheme manager and the old investors. Much like a pyramid scheme, there is a point where the new investor sign-up rate is unable to keep up with the demand of the investment returns for all the existing investors and the fraud is exposed. The fund then collapses as it is discovered that the "invested" capital is gone and, as in recent cases, was never ever invested.

Sam Israel of the Bayou Group used this approach and succeeded in getting $300 million from friends and friends of friends who decided to invest with him because of the reported excellent returns. The investors even included professional investment advisors who charge a fee for ensuring investment managers are credible and ethical by doing due diligence into the investment company's credibility. However, it seems that none of the investors and none of the investment advisors who recommended the fund bothered to check out Bayou's accounting firm, Richmond Fairfield Associates, which was charged with the independent audit of Bayou's transactions to ensure all performance claims were valid. If they had performed simple due diligence they would have discovered that Richmond Fairfield Associates was Israel's own firm and that the firm's address was merely a call center with an answering machine. For investors and investment advisors in New York City, a simple two dollar subway ride would have confirmed the nonexistence of an accredited accounting firm responsible for ensuring the validity of the fund's earnings reports. In the case of Bayou investors, their decisions to invest were emotion-based, triggered by the desire to join with other wealthy friends whom they assumed must have already done the due diligence required of any serious investment. Unfortunately, none had.

Similarly, Bernard Madoff, of Bernard Madoff Investment Securities, applied the same Ponzi approach to bilk investors and investment funds of $50 billion, including the money of his own sons, who eventually turned him in to the federal authorities. In like manner, Madoff selected Friehling & Horowitz as his accounting firm to conduct objective audits designed to protect the investors. Again, a simple visit to Friehling & Horowitz, located only about 30 miles from New York City, would have revealed an often empty one-room office that was clearly incapable of auditing $50 billion in securities transactions. Further, a basic review of the American

Institute of Certified Public Accountants (AICPA) records would have revealed that Friehling & Horowitz openly declared that they did not perform audits for clients. But no investor or investment advisor charged with doing due diligence for Madoff's clients ever bothered to check. Those advisors who did declined to invest. It is disturbing from these two examples that the investors and investment advisors failed to vet the investment managers and their accounting firms, which would have revealed troubling discoveries that would signal caution and further investigation. One of these embarrassed investment managers who had placed large sums with Madoff subsequently committed suicide.

An important lesson learned is that when making expert-based, fact-based, and probability-based decisions it is extremely important to verify the facts and probabilities that are driving the judgment criteria. Often they are not as represented. As President Ronald Reagan wisely proclaimed, "Trust but verify."

The Decision Solution Frame

The Decision Solution Frame Introduction

Earlier the decision type frame was defined, along with its four sides, to help understand the distinctions of decisions. It is repeated here as a reminder (see Figure 5.1).

The decision solution frame defines the distinctions of the candidate alternatives to be judged. The frame borders represent the boundaries of the limits and preferences for the considered alternatives. The area within the borders is called the solution trade space and is consistent with systems engineering trade study best practices. Alternatives that are excluded by the trade space boundaries are not considered, as they are properly screened out by the judgment criteria as being unacceptable. This simplifies

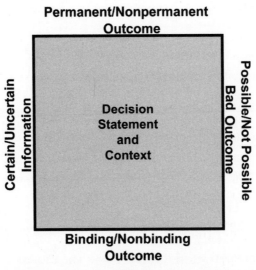

Figure 5.1   Decision Type Frame.

the alternative judgment process by not wasting time evaluating improbable alternatives.

The following is a representative list of decision frame content examples:

- Scope of the issue, such as deciding on a house design to be replicated in developments in multiple cities within the United States.

- Boundaries and limits, such as square footage, setbacks, height limits, and the like.

- Governing doctrine, including both legal doctrine and non-legal principles and guidelines.

- Ethics such as all codes, labor laws, and hiring practices that will be respected.

- Applicable and favored past experience.

- Personality influences such as Myers-Briggs profiles that may make certain criteria unacceptable to some stakeholders and may cause criteria weighting issues.

- Value profiles that quantify comparative criteria benefits over ranges of interest.

- In some cases the impact of addictive behavior may be suitable in the frame. For instance, a mandatory smoke-free environment can influence the alternatives considered.

The decision solution frame provides the boundaries for the candidate alternatives. For a vacation vehicle the solution frame might be as follows:

- Must be under $30,000
- Must get greater than 25 mpg
- Provide transportation for four to six vacations

- All-wheel drive
- Capable of towing camping trailer
- Reliable for five years of use
- Registered in California
- Attractive appearance to everyone
- Excellent media system
- High safety ratings

Note how each of these criterions will properly eliminate many noncompliant alternatives from consideration. Note also that without solution frame guidance the process would not focus exclusively on meaningful alternatives.

As a comparison, our vehicle selection example could be to decide on a vehicle to be used by the governor of California to demonstrate his "green, low carbon footprint." The frame and the associated alternatives for this challenge will be markedly different from those of the family vacation vehicle.

In the domain of systems engineering the decision solution frame is akin to the Concept of Operations (CONOPS) that defines the problem that any considered solution must satisfy the environments that it must operate in.

The frame should include hard factors such as size, weight, and dimensions. It can also contain qualitative factors such as ethics, personalities, attributes, and other difficult to articulate issues. Complicating these important solution guiding ingredients is the need to combine the interests of significant stakeholders. This will be the decision maker's most difficult task. Those who have held volunteer positions on community boards know this challenge all too well. By defining your decision trade space you will quickly and clearly surface which issues will require the most collaboration and negotiation among the stakeholders.

Decision Solution Frame Categories

The trade space boundaries include factors pertinent to the decision solution. Eight categories are offered but others may be equally or even more appropriate (see Figure 5.2). For instance, when deciding upon the attire for a formal function in a foreign land the customs of that culture should form a major part of the decision solution frame to ensure you do not embarrass your hosts or yourself by an inappropriate selection.

Care must be taken to include the most discriminating framing issues to ensure that only highly viable alternatives are considered.

Summaries of common solution trade space border categories are in the following subsections.

Scope and Limits

Scope defines the specified limits that should not be violated. As an example, if the decision relates to a new product it would be important to define the targeted buyer age range, their education level, the expected operating environments, the target market countries, and the timing of the introductions.

Limits make up the hard boundaries sometimes known as the "Musts" that must be complied with. They are "go" and "no go" boundaries. In construction projects limits might include building

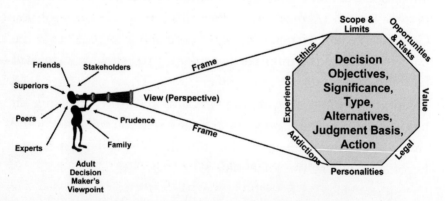

Figure 5.2   Decision Solution Frame.

setback dimensions and height limits. In automobiles they might include acceleration capability and stopping distances, and in finance limits might be credit scores and loan-to-value ratios.

Legal

Good decision making should be respectful of the laws governing the decision solution environment, considering the decision actions and consequences. The decision criteria should include applicable constraints so that the decision team is made aware of the bounding legal issues. As an example, when considering construction of a new home it is not uncommon to have multiple legal jurisdictions influencing the project's makeup such as county, city, and community agencies that include planning, building details, fire, public works, police protection, and so forth. In making international decisions there are often multiple and often conflicting legal issues that must be taken into consideration as part of the alternative judgment criteria.

Ethics

Ethics define the customs and conduct issues to assist in judging the acceptability of alternatives. Multinational customs are apt to introduce awkward ethical issues because of country to country inconsistencies as to what is considered reasonable and proper. Lockheed Aircraft Corporation was severely criticized several decades ago for bribing Japanese government officials to buy Lockheed airplanes during a time when it was considered normal to do so in some countries. Bribery is still considered normal and acceptable in some parts of the world.

Addictions

Addictions may influence considered alternatives when the objective is to support legal addictions (such as cigarette companies supporting those who smoke) or alternatives designed to reduce addictive behavior. Some people insist on bars and restaurants that permit smoking to satisfy their habit. Addictions may also become judgment criteria when the decision maker or decision team members are addicted to one alternative or some judgment criteria without fair evaluation of others and will guide the judgment criteria to bias to their favorite.

Experience

It is common and desirable for some decisions to be biased by the past experiences of the decision team. Judgment criteria often reflect these valuable experience-based biases. A danger is that creative alternatives may be precluded because they don't match the preconceived biases. This is sometimes called paradigm paralysis, which is a condition that inhibits the decision teams from being open and receptive to new and different alternatives and the decision solution frame is shaped to exclude them.

Personalities

The personalities of the stakeholders can have a significant effect on solution judging criteria. It is a formidable task to harness the diversity of stakeholder inputs into a cohesive and manageable set of constraints that bound the candidate solution alternatives. To comprehend and manage this challenge there are a number of useful personality type models to consider. Two of the more popular models are the Myers-Briggs Type Indicator (MBTI) and the Merrill-Reid or Merrill/Wilson four quadrant model. To keep this explanation simple, the more basic Merrill-Reid Model is referenced.

The first illustration (Figure 5.3) depicts the result of research that concluded personality types can be categorized into four basic types and then further characterized into 16 subtypes. A fairly

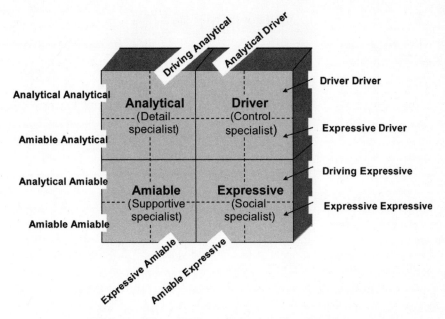

Figure 5.3 **Wilson Personality Model.**

simple questionnaire, completed by those who know the person being characterized, is used to determine a person's natural personality subtype. I am characterized as an Expressive/Driver, which seems correct. This is my fifth book, including three editions of my first book.

The four center subtypes identified in Figure 5.3, but not explained in the graphic are Amiable Driver, Analytical Expressive, Driving Amiable, and Expressive Analytical.

This expanded graphic of the Wilson Personality Model (Figure 5.4) lists the strengths and weaknesses for each of the general types. The sixteen blends draw from the associated characteristics.

From these characteristics it is easy to envision conflict between analytical (detail-oriented) stakeholders and expressive (undisciplined) stakeholders or between driver (decisive) stakeholders and amiable (noncommittal) stakeholders. It is the task of the decision-fit decision maker to develop consensus on the governing judgment

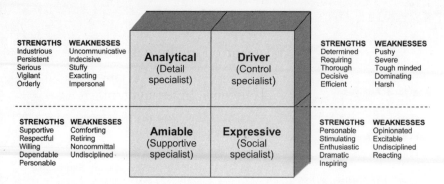

Figure 5.4 Wilson Personality Model—Detailed.

criteria, including those criteria that are personality driven. This challenge will test one's patience.

For instance, a Driver may rank return on investment as the most significant judgment criteria with the highest assigned weight. Simultaneously, the Amiable may seek to have environmentally friendly as the highest weighted constraint. A compatible compromise must be resolved.

A fit decision maker should also recognize his or her own personality biases and try to keep them from unfairly skewing the alternative judgment criteria.

Value

Value is a measure of the relative importance (comparative value) of alternative judgment criteria when compared to other criteria. Once the decision frame is defined the relative weighting among the criteria is beneficial and will aid in quantitative assessment of the alternatives. Some fact-based decision processes require that the alternatives be quantitatively scored against the weighted criteria based on how well the alternative satisfies the criteria. The score is then multiplied by the criteria weight to produce a weighted score that can then be compared with the weighted scores of competing alternatives. This will be discussed with fact-based alternative judging.

Opportunities and Their Risks

Decisions require the judgment of an alternative with a required action. Each alternative offers a different opportunity coupled with some inherent risk of a bad outcome. Investment information often includes a matrix that positions the recommended investment against both a benefit scale and a risk scale based on past performance so that the investor can determine if it is appropriate for inclusion into his or her portfolio. The opportunity benefit to risk ratio or risk tolerance is a personal and often an emotional judgment and in team decision making requires skillful collaboration to achieve group consensus regarding the team's combined opportunity/risk motivation and tolerance.

There is a long needed clarification about risk management. For decades our country has been risk-centric and has cultivated risk management books, associations, conferences, and software. We encourage the taking of risks and we speak of risks often. But we have become so risk intense that we often focus on risk to the exclusion of opportunity.

But America is the land of opportunity, and in spite of that we scarcely hear of opportunity management in our business and personal lives. Managers and leaders often speak of "taking risk," but if that was responded to literally there would be high criticism. One can take a risk by jumping off the Golden Gate Bridge, but it would have no opportunity justifying purpose unless it is suicide.

A Google search of risk management reveals almost 43 million hits. Given the great opportunities we have in the United States, we should be opportunity-centric to feed our innovative culture. Yet a similar search of opportunity management only results in 490,000 hits—almost a 100:1 ratio in favor of risk management to opportunity management. This disappointing disparity is caused by our flawed jargon, which continues to encourage people to take risk when the intent is for them to seek and pursue opportunities. We witness this flawed communication on *American Idol* and *America's Got Talent* almost every season when the judges frequently suggest that the contestants "take risk" when they really mean for them to seek new opportunities to excel and to show what their full capabilities are.

There is no risk on the planet that has not been caused by the pursuit of a parent opportunity. We need to keep the parent opportunity connected to its risk and we need to manage them in tandem. To manage one without the other is shortsighted and ineffective. The better paradigm is to *manage opportunities and their risks*.

The Impact of Uncertainty

Most of life's decisions will be fact-based if we are diligent enough to seek the relevant facts. Internet resources provide enormous amounts of up-to-date data that we can quickly and easily access and apply. Unfortunately, in the haste to make a decision, decision makers often ignore the readily available information and make judgments based on emotion or intuition, leading to snap judgment.

When decision criteria include degrees of uncertainty, as in decisions that have to do with unpredictable future events, then estimates of that uncertainty must be made. However, research has shown that humans are very unreliable when making estimates in unfamiliar regions, which in turn can lead to faulty judgment. This aspect will be treated further in Chapter 8, about probability-based decisions.

Developing Alternatives and Related Information (Facts and Probabilities)

Alternatives considered for judgment should pass an initial screening to eliminate those that have no chance of succeeding, with the result that any of the remaining alternatives could be acceptable. In car selection this would rule out styles, colors, and even brands that would not be acceptable even if judged superior. Internet searches can provide timely, relevant information leading to viable alternatives and comparative facts. For consumer items there are many reliable websites that provide both expert analysis and owner's reports. *Consumer Reports'* website is one of the most popular, rating both products and services. *Car and Driver* and *Motor Trend* both provide extensive analysis of automobiles. The website www.edmunds.com provides both expert analysis and owner reports on all available automobiles. A recent check of my wife's car provides 69 owner reports detailing their positive and negative experiences as owners. My car, which is older, has 113 owner's reports. The advantage of these ongoing reports is that they are usually up-to-date and reflect the owner's experiences over time. The professional product raters only report once and usually at the introduction of a product so they are unable to report on experiences over time and with increasing mileage.

There are other car rating sites, such as J.D. Power and MSN; just search Google *car ratings* and scroll down from there.

Information on consumer products is just as readily available.

The following is a candidate list of product rating websites:

www.buzzillions.com

http://www.product-reviews.net

www.cnet.com

www.audioreview.com

www.reviewcentre.com

www.consumerreview.com

www.amazon.com

www.epinions.com

www.projectorreviews.com

www.review.zdnet.com

These websites can provide both alternatives for consideration in your selection process and the associated data to facilitate side-by-side comparison against your defined judgment criteria. Some of these sites provide the capability for instant side-by-side comparison of competing alternatives.

The Internet can also provide other important decision data. For instance, the websites www.census.gov/prod/2002pubs/p23-210.pdf and www.womenscouncil.org/documents/FAQs/Education_percent 20and_percent20Earnings.pdf provide the lifetime economic impact of levels of education. This is valuable data to consider when facing the decision to further one's education.

Another valuable website, www.fda.gov/consumer/features/tattoos 120607.html, provides data on the risks of tattoos. Since the tattoo business and the tattoo processes are unregulated, significant health risks are present that are usually not disclosed to tattoo clients.

We are often challenged by important decisions regarding illness diagnosis and doctor-ordered remedies in the form of prescriptions and other methods. The Internet provides enough information that it can almost serve as the basis for a second opinion. Searches of an identified illness can provide opinions and testimonials of those with similar symptoms and circumstances. Searches of prescribed medications can provide both the benefits and side effects that can assist in the determination of adopting a recommendation. The following are some sites offering medication information:

www.viewpoints.com/Prescription-Medicine

www.drugratingz.com/

www.consumersearch.com/diet-pills/prescription-diet-pills

In some cases Internet searches can provide probability factors where past history establishes a credible reference, especially with regard to future weather and such things as expected stock market performance related to election years and election year results. The Internet is not a good resource for probability estimates where no past history exists, as in the probability of success of new drugs, surgical procedures, or unproven technology.

PART

II

Deciding

Process-Assisted Judgment

What Type of Decision Is It?

At this point you should now be sufficiently decision fit to be able to characterize your decisions based on the following questions.

1. Is there a potential for a seriously negative outcome?
2. Can the decision lead to a permanent outcome?
3. Is there considerable uncertainty in the information that the judgment must be based upon?
4. Does the judgment lead to a binding agreement with others that must be respected?

If you can declare four "No" responses for these questions your decision is of low consequence and almost any alternative judgment basis will do. However, to ensure a quality judgment you may benefit by applying one of the fact-based processes that follow. If your analysis results in four "Yes" responses, the decision is highly significant and deserves the ultimate rigor in analysis and process to ensure the best course of action is selected. Other combinations of results will cause you to consider more or less rigor in the judgment process.

Some decision judgments are easy, especially when a single alternative clearly stands out as superior to all others. This is sometimes the case in selecting a house, a car, or a vacation. For instance, if you want to select a new all-wheel drive minivan the decision is simple since Toyota is currently the only supplier with their AWD Toyota Sienna. All other manufacturers have abandoned all-wheel drive minivans.

If you desire a five bedroom waterfront house in California with a 100-foot dock the inventory is very limited and the judgment should be relatively simple selecting from the few available.

Often decisions involve many candidate alternatives, with the superiority of one over another not easily discernible. This is especially true in the selection of an SUV from those available. The April 2011 edition of *Consumer Reports* lists 94 different SUVs to consider. The selection of a college to attend can be similarly challenging. For these complex decisions the following fact-based and probability-based processes can be valuable to distinguish among "good, better, and best" according to your carefully crafted solution frame judgment criteria.

Alternative Judgment Methods

A decision is the judgment and selection of an alternative resulting in action. This selection can be based on any of the 10 bases of judgment, ranging from indifference and applying the flip of a coin to probability-based decisions requiring exhaustive investigation and experimentation to minimize potential inaccuracies in probability estimates.

Indifference-based, addiction-based, faith-based, emotion-based, and some pressure-based decisions need little decision analysis. The decision maker decides the judgment of the alternatives using any of these bases and proclaims the action without detailed justification, as none is called for or expected when these methods are used. They are based on personal perception and values. Decision makers may exclaim that they "like" one alternative over another, or that they have a "feeling" about their favorite alternative without consciously realizing that their judgment is being based on emotion, intuition, or some sort of pressure. Addiction-based decision makers will usually tenaciously cling to one alternative without offering a logical explanation.

However, doctrine-based, expert-based, fact-based, and probability-based decisions often require explanation of the decision rationale, especially when defending a selected action to others such as to an authority or in a court of law. There are multiple alternative

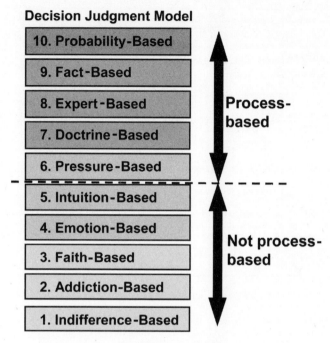

Figure 6.1   Decision Judgment Model.

judgment processes with varying degrees of rigor. Several of these processes follow. Although not an exact science, the rigor and analytical complexity of the judgment process tends to increase in progression from bottom to top (see Figure 6.1).

Figure 6.2 provides the road map that will be followed regarding business defensible judgment methods.

Process-Based Judgments

From bottom to top, Figure 6.2 identifies 10 process-based judgment methods that can be defended when challenged by others.

The first in the series, pressure based, can be defended if the pressure is by legitimate authority and the judgment process is directed at proving the legitimacy of the authority. This requires due diligence

Type	Name	Characteristics
Probability-Based	Bayesian Team Support Process	Requires experts with beliefs, alternatives, preferences, and ongoing updates
	Decision Tree Process	Requires uncertainty estimates and outcome value knowledge
Fact-Based	Analytical Hierarchy Process (AHP)	Pairwise weighting, pairwise scores, weighted scores, and other factors
	Kepner-Tregoe (KT) Derived Process	Prioritization, weighted scores, and other factors
	Pugh's Process	Prioritize, weight, and rate
	Dominance Analysis Process	Compliance table and even swaps
	Rank Sums Process	Criteria ranking sums
Expert-Based	Expert Judgment Process	Informed judgment by vetted expert
Doctrine-Based	Rules Govern Process	By the book. May be legal driven
Pressure-Based	Authority Judgment Process	Authority knows best. Not peers and perks

Figure 6.2   Defensible Judgments Road Map.

to confirm the credibility and the vested power of the authority. This process might require the engagement of a private investigator or a consultant who performs background investigations if the decision warrants that type of effort. Most investment scams, including Ponzi schemes and other rip-offs, would have been discovered by the application of formal background investigations.

Doctrine-based judgment requires the analysis necessary to determine the documented criteria that are appropriate to the decision at hand. Court case decisions are usually based on applicable laws and whether they were violated. In nonlegal situations it is important to amass the relevant codes of conduct and regulations that influence the alternatives available and come to consensus as to which will apply to govern the judgment. When dealing with international situations and where multiple jurisdictions may prevail, determining the relevant doctrine-based rules may be difficult.

It is noteworthy that one of the most advanced surveillance satellite systems ever developed was cancelled before completion. One reason was that it had thousands of soldered connections fabricated with solder that contained tin, which was found in the 1960s to cause the growth of conductive whiskers over time that then could produce short circuits and ultimate catastrophic spacecraft failure. While this doctrine recorded rule was carried throughout the industry for decades in both government specifications and company procedures, it was absent in the most recent documentation, and the process engineers were too new to know of the past failures and the resulting rule. This oversight contributed to the wasting of billions of dollars.

Expert-based judgment requires little detailed analysis by the decision maker, but does require full due diligence in the vetting of the expert including background checks to provide necessary justification as to why the expert(s) are credible to make the decision judgment. This may require comprehensive experience checks, reference verifications, and personal credibility statements signed by the experts to ensure their qualifications and experience are applicable to the required judgment. As an example, there have been instances where noncertified, noneducated persons misrepresented themselves as doctors and actually performed surgery and other medical procedures on unsuspecting patients with undesirable outcomes. Proper due diligence should have revealed this illegal practice.

The summary in Figure 6.3 is an example of this point.

- Gerald Barnes repeatedly posed as a medical doctor.
- His lack of knowledge contributed to the death of John McKenzie.
- He plea-bargained to manslaughter and served 19 months.
- While on bail, Barnes practiced medicine fraudulently.
- Served three more prison sentences.
- Later he got a job performing physical checkups on FBI agents.
- During a prison transfer Barnes escaped and was found working as a physician.
- Now serving a 20-year sentence.

Figure 6.3   Lack of Due Diligence Example.

Because of the current high incidence of medical decision errors, everyone should have a strong and aggressive advocate to ensure that medical treatments, prescribed drugs, and food being administered within and by a medical organization are all correct. It is all too common for medical staff to get patients and their treatments mixed up. This is another proper application of President Reagan's "trust but verify" code of conduct.

Expert judgment in nonmedical areas such as automobiles, electronics, software, and so forth, is often sought. There are experts who can provide decision judgment assistance in almost any field. Internet searches can provide valuable relevant information about possible causes of symptoms in almost any field with recommended solutions. Entering the exact error message or the exact symptoms into a browser search will often result in a recommended action that works.

The website www.yelp.com provides user feedback on many service organizations. This tool can provide valuable access to an "expert's credibility," but be wary of self-created feedback. Look for a significantly high number of positive results that are too large to have been self-entered.

CHAPTER 7

Fact-Based Judgment

Fact-Based Judgment, aka Low Uncertainty Judgments

There are decisions where the facts relative to a judgment favor one alternative so that no rigorous analysis is required. There are other decisions where there is no clear superior alternative and the competing alternatives must be analyzed against multiple judgment criteria to determine the overall "best" choice. In these cases fact-based judgment can be determined logically by applying a judgment process to the competing alternatives. There are five popular processes for fact-based judgment (see Figure 7.1). These five processes are covered in the order of increasing thoroughness, each improving on the prior.

Rank Sums Judgment Process

As illustrated in Figure 7.2 Rank Sums is the first of the fact-based processes to be described. Rank sums judgment is the most basic of fact-based judgment and is mostly a qualitative process. It is

Type	Name	Characteristics
Fact-Based	Analytical Hierarchy Process (AHP)	Pair wise prioritization, weighted scores, and other factors
	Kepner-Tregoe (KT) Derived Process	Prioritization, weighted scores, and other factors
	Pugh's Process	Prioritize, weight, and rate
	Dominance Analysis Process	Compliance table and even swaps
	Rank Sums Process	Criteria ranking sums

We are here

Figure 7.1   Fact-Based Road Map.

Type	Name	Characteristics
Fact-Based	Analytical Hierarchy Process (AHP)	Pairwise prioritization, weighted scores, and other factors
	Kepner-Tregoe (KT) Derived Process	Prioritization, weighted scores, and other factors
	Pugh's Process	Prioritize, weight, and rate
	Dominance Analysis Process	Compliance table and even swaps
	Rank Sums Process	**Criteria ranking sums**

Figure 7.2   Rank Sums Process.

quick, simple, and easy to explain. For this process all of the judgment criteria are considered equal so criteria weights and weighted score calculations are not applied. (Weights and weighted scores are explained later in this chapter.) Instead, each of the alternatives is sequentially ranked in the order that they satisfy each judgment criterion, with one being the best and therefore the highest ranking. In this process it is permissible to have tie or equal rankings for a criterion. The alternatives' rankings for all criterion are then summed to determine the lowest score, which identifies the overall highest ranked considering the rankings of all of the criteria, and therefore the best selection.

The chart of Figure 7.3 illustrates the basis of the Rank Sums Process. While this process is quick and easy, there are issues that may be significant to your application. Since the process assumes that all criteria are of equal weight (equal importance), the results may differ if the criteria were weighted. If you apply this process and the results reveal two alternatives that are close in total score you should apply weighting to the criteria to determine if one alternative is significantly better than the other when weighting is considered. If not, then emotion-based final judgment may be applied to determine the final selection.

Criterion/Alt	Alt #1	Alt #2	Alt #3	Alt #4
Criterion #1	4	2	1	3
Criterion #2	1	1	1	1
Criterion #3	3	2	1	4
Criterion #4	1	2	2	2
Criterion #5	4	4	1	2
Criterion #6	3	1	2	3
Criterion #7	3	2	1	2
Criterion #8	3	2	1	3
TOTAL	22	16	10	20

Alternative #3 has the lowest score and is the highest ranked (best choice) – Like a golf score.

Figure 7.3 Rank Sums Ranking Table Example.

Figure 7.4 is a real example using current published comparative data. The challenge is the evaluation of five family sedan alternatives. The alternative names have been disguised. All comparative data were derived from readily available Internet sources. Note that the fuel efficiency is measured in the U.S. standard of miles

Criterion/Alt	Brand #1	Brand #2	Brand #3	Brand #4	Brand #5
Price	3	5	1	2	4
Seating	1	1	1	1	1
HP	2	4	5	3	1
Trans Speeds	1	2	2	1	1
Fuel Type	1	1	1	1	1
mpg	1	1	2	3	1
0–60	3	4	5	2	1
61–0	3	4	1	3	2
Trunk	4	5	1	3	2
Turn radius	2	4	1	5	3
Reliability	2	1	3	4	3
Total	23	32	23	28	20

Figure 7.4 Rank Sums—Small Sedan Criteria Ranking.

per gallon (mpg), where a higher number is better as contrasted to the European standard of gallons per mile (or liters per kilometer), where a lower number is better.

In this example Brand 5 is a clear winner, enjoying almost a 15 percent advantage over the nearest competitor. If the results were close then test driving the close competitors would allow the emotional basis to influence the final judgment.

Dominance Analysis Judgment Process

Dominance analysis is another qualitative judgment process that can produce satisfactory results (see Figure 7.5). It is based on the progressive elimination of alternatives that are judged subordinate to others that are superior. An advantage is that it provides for and encourages trading off disparate criteria when deemed by the decision maker to be relatively equivalent in value. By successively trading off "equivalents" the decision criteria are progressively eliminated and reduced to a few remaining driving criteria which are simpler to comprehend and manage. This process is highly judgmental and the judgment of the decision maker may not be shared by all stakeholders.

Type	Name	Characteristics
Fact-Based	Analytical Hierarchy Process (AHP)	Pair wise prioritization, weighted scores, and other factors
	Kepner-Tregoe (KT) Derived Process	Prioritization, weighted scores, and other factors
	Pugh's Process	Prioritize, weight, and rate
	Dominance Analysis Process	**Compliance table and even swaps**
	Rank Sums Process	Criteria ranking sums

Figure 7.5   Dominance Analysis Process.

The vacation selection example in Figure 7.6 illustrates the process. The first step is to construct a consequence table that facilitates comparison of each alternative's capability for each of the criteria. The family has identified the parameters important to their judgment and have listed them in their consequence table. The advantage of the consequence table is that it facilitates a variety of response comparisons from quantitative to qualitative and subjective. In this first illustration Vacation 1 is immediately judged inferior to all of the others and is discarded as noncompetitive because of poor weather, inconvenience, and museums as the only points of interest.

Criterion/Alt	Vacation #1	Vacation #2	Vacation #3	Vacation #4
Cost/Person	$2,000	$3,000	$5,000	$6,000
Weather	Fair	Good	Good	Excellent
Sports	Many	Several	Few	Many
Food	Buffet	Menu	Menu	Gourmet
Amenities	3	5	8	10
Travel Required	Inconvenient	Convenient	Convenient	Inconvenient
Points of Interest	Museums	Scenic	Scenic	Various

Vacation #1 is dominated and is eliminated because of poor weather, inconvenient travel, and limitation to museums.

Figure 7.6   Dominance Compliance Table—Eliminate dominated alternatives.

Next, Vacation 4 is discarded from further evaluation due to inconvenient travel and high cost (see Figure 7.7).

Criterion/Alt	Vacation #2	Vacation #3	Vacation #4
Cost/Person	$3,000	$5,000	$6,000
Weather	Good	Good	Excellent
Sports	Several	Few	Many
Food	Menu	Menu	Gourmet
Amenities	5	8	10
Travel Required	Convenient	Convenient	Inconvenient
Points of Interest	Scenic	Scenic	Various

Vacation #4 is dominated and is eliminated because of inconvenient travel and high cost.

Figure 7.7   Dominance Compliance Table—Eliminate dominated alternatives.

The next step is to remove judgment criteria that have consequences judged by the decision maker to be roughly equivalent. In
this example, weather, food, travel, and points of interest are now
considered equal for the remaining alternatives (see Figure 7.8).

Criterion/Alt	Vacation #2	Vacation #3
Cost/Person	$3,000	$5,000
~~Weather~~	~~Good~~	~~Good~~
Sports	Several	Few
~~Food~~	~~Menu~~	~~Menu~~
Amenities	5	8
~~Travel Required~~	~~Convenient~~	~~Convenient~~
~~Points of Interest~~	~~Scenic~~	~~Scenic~~

**Figure 7.8   Dominance Compliance Table—Eliminate criteria
with near equal responses.**

The final step is to make even swaps or "trades," where the consequences are considered by the decision maker to be approximately
equivalent (see Figure 7.9).

The dominance analysis process has reduced the judgment to
only the cost criteria of the remaining two alternatives. Dominance
analysis Vacation 2 is based on the best choice.

Criterion/Alt	Vacation #2	Vacation #3
Cost/Person	$3,000	$5,000
~~Sports~~	~~Some~~	~~Few~~
~~Amenities~~	~~5~~	~~8~~

Considered equivalent value and an "equal swap"

More sports on Vacation #2 is considered an "equal swap" for more
amenities on Vacation #3 leaving cost as the sole driver of the judgment.

**Figure 7.9   Dominance Compliance Table—Eliminate criteria
pairs approximately equivalent.**

The second example (Figure 7.10) of the dominance analysis process is based on the earlier rank sums family sedan judgment example. Keep in mind that this is a subjective process based on the assessments of the decision maker.

Criterion/Alt	Brand #1	Brand #2	Brand #3	Brand #4	Brand #5
Price	$28,020	$31,090	$23,345	$23,945	$28,400
Seating	5	5	5	5	5
HP	268	244	234	252	270
Trans Speeds	6	5	5	6	Contin
Fuel Type	Regular	Regular	Regular	Regular	Regular
mpg	23	23	21	20	23
0-60	7.1	7.3	7.5	6.6	6.4
60-0	137	142	132	137	136
Trunk	14.5	14	16.3	14.9	15.3
Turn radius	36.1	39.6	35.8	40.4	37.4
Reliability	14.5	15	13.5	No data	13.5

Figure 7.10   Dominance Compliance Table—Car Example.

For this example, the first step is to eliminate the equivalent consequences (see Figure 7.11). Seating and fuel type are identical for all alternatives and can immediately be eliminated from further consideration. In addition, the decision maker has concluded that the transmissions, while slightly different in two of the cases, are judged equivalent and can be eliminated as judgment criteria.

Criterion/Alt	Brand #1	Brand #2	Brand #3	Brand #4	Brand #5
Price	$28,020	$31,090	$23,345	$23,945	$28,400
~~Seating~~	~~5~~	~~5~~	~~5~~	~~5~~	~~5~~
HP	268	244	234	252	270
~~Trans Speeds~~	~~6~~	~~5~~	~~5~~	~~6~~	~~Contin~~
~~Fuel Type~~	~~Regular~~	~~Regular~~	~~Regular~~	~~Regular~~	~~Regular~~
mpg	23	23	21	20	23
0-60	7.1	7.3	7.5	6.6	6.4
60-0	137	142	132	137	136
Trunk	14.5	14	16.3	14.9	15.3
Turn radius	36.1	39.6	35.8	40.4	37.4
Reliability	14.5	15	13.5	No data	13.5

Figure 7.11   Dominance Compliance Table—Eliminate criteria with near equal compliance.

Now the obviously dominated alternatives can be eliminated from further consideration (see Figure 7.12).

Criterion/Alt	Brand #1	Brand #2	Brand #3	Brand #4	Brand #5
Price	$28,020	$31,090	$23,345	$23,945	$28,400
Seating	5	5	5	5	5
mpg	23	23	21	20	23
0-60	7.1	7.3	7.5	6.6	6.4
60-0	137	142	132	137	136
Trunk	14.5	14	16.3	14.9	15.3
Turn radius	36.1	39.6	35.8	40.4	37.4
Reliability	14.5	15	13.5	No data	13.5

High price,
bad braking,
large radius

Poor mpg,
large radius,
suspect
reliability

Figure 7.12 Dominance Compliance Table—Eliminate dominated alternatives.

Brand 2 is dominated and eliminated because it is high priced, has low horsepower, is slow on acceleration, is long on stopping, and has a large turning radius. Brand 4 is dominated and eliminated because of its unknown reliability, its large turning radius, and its low gas mileage.

The next step is to eliminate remaining criteria by trading or swapping criteria that are judged to be approximately equivalent and also by eliminating relatively unimportant criteria to the final judgment.

In Figure 7.13 the fuel mileage and the trunk space are considered equal since the lower fuel mileage car had the largest trunk and the other cars with higher fuel mileage had smaller trunks. The criteria of 60-0 braking and reliability are viewed as approximately equivalent for all cars and are eliminated as judgment drivers.

Criterion/Alt	Brand #1		Brand #3		Brand #5
Price	$28,020		$23,345		$28,400
Seating	5		5		5
~~mpg~~	~~23~~		~~21~~		~~23~~
0-60	7.1		7.5		6.4
~~60-0~~	~~187~~		~~182~~		~~186~~
~~Trunk~~	~~14.5~~		~~16.3~~		~~15.3~~
Turn radius	36.1		35.8		37.4
~~Reliability~~	~~14.5~~		~~13.5~~		~~13.5~~

mpg and trunk size results considered equivalent.

Braking and reliability results considered equivalent.

Figure 7.13 Dominance Compliance Table—Eliminate near equal criteria pairs.

The next step is to judge based on value (benefit/cost) of the remaining alternatives. Brand 3 in this example is the lowest price by far, has the best turning radius, and has acceptable acceleration (see Figure 7.14).

Criterion/Alt	Brand #1		Brand #3		Brand #5
Price	$28,020		$23,345		$28,400
Seating	5		5		5
0-60	7.1		7.5		6.4
Turn radius	36.1		35.8		37.4
			Low price and good performance		

Figure 7.14 Dominance Compliance Table—Judge based on value.

Note again that this is not an exact science. Brand 3, the best value selection by the dominance analysis process, was second-best when judged using the rank sums process.

Pugh's Judgment Process

Pugh's Process is the first step toward judgment of alternatives using quantitative analysis (see Figure 7.15). In this method the judgment criteria are weighted as to their importance and the alternatives are compared to a reference standard as to being better or worse than the reference standard. If better, the alternative being judged receives a plus and if worse it receives a minus. A zero is applied when the alternative is judged equivalent to the reference standard. To determine the "best" alternative the weighted pluses and the weighted minuses are summed to reveal a total weighted score for each alternative. In this process the highest (best) score determines the selection. As discussed earlier, if the results show close scoring between one or more alternatives then emotion-based judgment may be appropriate to make the final determination.

Type	Name	Characteristics
	Analytical Hierarchy Process (AHP)	Pairwise prioritization, weighted scores, and other factors
	Kepner-Tregoe (KT) Derived Process	Prioritization, weighted scores, and other factors
Fact-Based	**Pugh's Process**	**Prioritize, weight, and rate**
	Dominance Analysis Process	Compliance table and even swaps
	Rank Sums Process	Criteria ranking sums

Figure 7.15   Pugh's Process.

Criterion/Alt	Weight	Reference	Concept #1	Concept #2
Size	10	0	0	+
Weight	9	0	+	+
Proc time	9	0	+	+
Performance	8	0	+	−
Perf margin	6	0	+	−
Reliability	6	0	+	−
Risk	6	0	−	+
Cost	5	0	−	−
Training	5	0	0	+
Sparing	4	0	−	+
Total +		0	+5 (38)	+6 (43)
Total −		0	−3 (15)	−4 (25)
Total		0	+2 (23)	+2 (18)

23   vs.   18

Figure 7.16 Pugh's Compliance Table—Judge based on weighted minus and plus sums.

In this basic Pugh's Process example shown in Figure 7.16, Concept 1 is judged better than the reference five times with two weights of nine, one of eight, and two of six totaling 38 positive points. Concept 1 also has three minuses compared to the reference with weights of six, five, and four resulting in a negative 15 points to be applied to the plus 38 points, producing a Concept 1 total of 23 points. Concept 2, using the same arithmetic process, yields plus 43 and minus 25 for a net total of 18 points. Concept 1 is judged superior by five points ($23-18=5$).

The second Pugh's Process example refers again to the prior family vehicle evaluation (see Figure 7.17).

Criterion/Alt	Wgt	Std	Brand #1	Brand #2	Brand #3	Brand #4	Brand #5
Price	10	25,000	−	−	+	+	−
Seating	10	5	0	0	0	0	0
HP	4	250	+	−	−	+	+
Trans	4	5	+	0	0	+	+
Fuel Type	8	Regular	0	0	0	0	0
mpg	10	22	+	+	−	−	+
0-60	8	7	−	−	−	+	+
60-0	8	140	+	−	+	+	+
Trunk	8	15	−	−	+	−	+
Turn radius	8	38	+	−	+	−	+
Reliability	10	13	+	+	+	−	+
Total			18	−26	30	−2	50

Figure 7.17 Pugh's Compliance Table Car Example—Judge based on weighted minus and plus sums.

As stated this process requires the establishment of a reference standard and the magnitude of the better or worse comparisons to the standard is not considered. It is interesting to note that using the Pugh Process, results in Brand 5 being judged superior, confirming the earlier Rank Sums finding. Brand 3, which was judged best by the Dominance Analysis Process is second here. Again, this disparity is a result of the subjective nature of the processes and the inability to quantify and provide credit for much better than and much worse than performances compared to the reference. That deficiency will be accommodated by the KT Derived Process and the Analytical Hierarchy Process (AHP) which are discussed in the remainder of this chapter of fact-based decision processes. The KT and AHP processes are mathematically rigorous, although straightforward, and are perhaps more useful for application to critical investment, business, medical, engineering, and other decisions. Readers may want to skip to Chapter 8 on probability-based decision making and return to complete this chapter later.

Kepner-Tregoe Derived Judgment Process (KT)

This Kepner-Tregoe Derived Process is a widely applied and well-respected method of alternative judgment (see Figure 7.18). Criteria

Type	Name	Characteristics
	Analytical Hierarchy Process (AHP)	Pairwise prioritization, weighted scores, and other factors
Fact-Based	**Kepner-Tregoe (KT) Derived Process**	**Prioritization, weighted scores, and other factors**
	Pugh's Process	Prioritize, weight, and rate
	Dominance Analysis Process	Compliance table and even swaps
	Rank Sums Process	Criteria ranking sums

Figure 7.18   Kepner-Tregoe Derived Process.

can be both quantitative and qualitative and are weighted with respect to one another. Alternatives are judged and scored as to how well they satisfy the criteria to yield weighted scores. The KT Derived Process also includes "Other Factors Analysis" that facilitates, including late-breaking news, previously not considered (overlooked) factors, and potential adverse consequences (risk) to finally influence the ultimate judgment. The flow diagram in Figure 7.19 illustrates the KT Derived Process, which is sometimes called the trade study process in technical disciplines such as systems engineering.

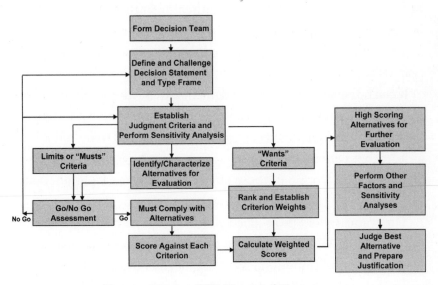

Figure 7.19   KT Derived Process.

The first step in the KT Derived Process is to form the decision team and to identify the decision maker. The decision maker and the team should be decision fit—skilled in the process, emotionally centered, and up to the decision challenge.

Next determine the decision objectives, decision statement, decision context, decision type frame, and decision solution frame that form the judgment criteria. This is the point where the decision statement is challenged by the decision maker to get it as correct as possible. The decision of "What car should I buy?" might be improved by deciding "What vehicle should I acquire?" or "What transportation should I use?" The decision solution frame should set the boundaries of the trade space of the alternatives, such as specifying that the transportation is to be used for both business and pleasure, which includes camping for six and towing of a 4,000-pound boat in the state of California.

The alternative judgment criteria are established with both the musts and weighted "wants." Musts are mandatory, quantitative, and binary in nature. They are either satisfied by an alternative or they are not. If they are not, the alternative is discarded from any further evaluation. For example, "must weigh less than 5,000 pounds" can be a mandatory quantitative criterion.

It can be beneficial to have a judgment criterion represented by both a must and a want relative to a single judgment issue. For instance, a must of at least 20 miles per gallon will eliminate all that do not have at least that performance. Then, a want of high gasoline mileage will give beneficial scoring to those alternatives that exceed the 20 mpg minimum, with higher scores going to the better performing.

The wants should be assigned weights proportional to the priority of the criteria. Wants can be criteria that are either quantitative and measurable or subjective and requiring judgment in the quantification of the scoring. Typically in the KT Derived Process the most important want receives a weight of 10; other wants are compared to the most important and receive weights proportional to their influence on the judging. It is acceptable to have multiple criteria with the same weight. Before approving the weighted criteria, a sensitivity assessment should be made to evaluate the proportional influence that the criteria have on the planned judgment. If it is discovered that the weights are out of proportion (too high on visual appearance, for instance) the weights should be adjusted to ensure appropriate proportional influence. An example of sensitivity analysis is shown in Figure 7.20.

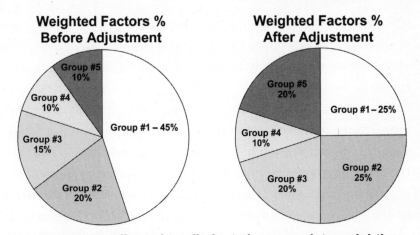

Note: **Weights are adjusted to eliminate inappropriate weighting.**

Figure 7.20   Sensitivity Analysis Example.

The next step following the establishment of the judgment criteria is to conceive the alternatives for evaluation. Brainstorming and other creative thinking methods are appropriate to meet this challenge. Teams should look for diverse alternatives that have the potential for satisfying the criteria. Care should be exercised to avoid the temptation to select alternatives that are simply variants of another. Once the alternatives have been identified and characterized, the judgment process can proceed.

All alternatives are compared to the must criteria and any that fail are discarded from further evaluation, leaving only the remaining for scoring and weighted scoring. In the scoring process one popular approach is to score the alternative that best satisfies a criterion a 10 and then compare how other alternatives satisfy the same criterion in comparison to the best and score it proportionally. As an example, an alternative that only satisfies a criterion half as well as the best would get a score of five. A second scoring process is to define a reference standard where the standards for a 10 score are defined and all alternatives are compared and scored against the reference standard. It is advisable to avoid excessive precision. This is a process that is based on informed judgment to eliminate substandard alternatives and to surface a few of the best for further evaluation.

When alternative scoring has been completed the criteria scores and the criteria weights are multiplied to produce a weighted score for each criterion for each alternative. Then the weighted scores are added for each alternative to achieve a total weighted score. Typically there will be alternatives earning low weighted scores that are then discarded from further evaluation. There are often several high scores within 10 percent to 15 percent of each other, and these are considered alternatives for further evaluation since the weighted scoring process is not an exact science.

Other Factors Analysis encourages consideration of factors that may not have been thought of in the evaluation, new information that has emerged during the decision analysis process, and potential adverse consequences. For instance, in the selection of a vehicle a new *Consumer Reports* edition may show recently discovered poor reliability of the highest scoring vehicle that was not known or considered during the evaluation. (For example, spontaneous acceleration of Toyotas.) This new information may be significant enough to eliminate a high scoring contender from selection. Other Factors Analysis facilitates the consideration of late-breaking news in much the same way as that incorporated in the Bayesian Team Support Process, which will be discussed later.

Based on the weighted scoring analysis and the Other Factors Analysis, informed judgment can be made and documented, including the logic that led to the conclusion.

Figure 7.21 is a typical Kepner-Tregoe Derived Process Table.

Decision Statement:

Evaluation Criteria:	Weight	Alternative 1			Alternative 2			Alternative 3			Alternative 4		
		Comments	Raw (R)	R*W	Comments	Raw (R)	R*W	Comments	Raw (R)	R*W	Comments	Raw (R)	R*W
			Score			Score			Score			Score	
Musts (Go/No-Go):													
Wants:													
Max Score (10xW):													
Total Score:													

Figure 7.21   KT Derived Process Table.

Figure 7.22 is a completed example for the selection of a car to meet a family's decision criteria.

Decision Statement:	Select the best vehicle to meet the needs of the Jones family. (Mom, Dad, and three kids, ages 5 to 16)												
Evaluation Criteria:		Alternative 1 Car			Alternative 2 Pickup Truck			Alternative 3 Minivan			Alternative 4 SUV		
Musts (Go/No-Go):													
Less than $35,000		Y			Y			Y			N		
Transport five people		Y			N			Y			Y		
Wants:	Weight	Comments	Score Raw (R)	R*W	Comments	Score Raw (R)	R*W	Comments	Score Raw (R)	R*W	Comments	Score Raw (R)	R*W
Fuel economy	8	26.2 mpg	10	80				20.0 mpg	6	48			
Good acceleration	6	10.5 sec	3	18				7.0 sec	10	60			
Crash safety	10	High Ratings	10	100				Avg. Ratings	7	63			
Carry garden supplies	9	Small cap	2	18				Large Cap	10	100			
Good for dates (16 yr.)	4	"Cool image"	10	40				Conservative	6	24			
Max Score (10xW):	370												
Total Score:				256						295			

Max Score = Sum of Weights X 10
May wish to "normalize" so that max score is 100 or 1,000

Figure 7.22   KT Derived Process Example.

Some decision analysts prefer scores relative to a standard number such as 100 or 1,000. If normalizing is applied to adjust scores relative to a maximum possible score of a round number such as 1,000 the following summary results (see Figure 7.23). The decision is not altered as the results change proportionally.

Decision Statement:	Select the best vehicle to meet the needs of the Jones family. (Mom, Dad, and three kids, ages 5 to 16)												
Evaluation Criteria:		Alternative 1 Car			Alternative 2 Pickup Truck			Alternative 3 Minivan			Alternative 4 SUV		
Musts (Go/No-Go):													
Less than $35,000		Y			Y			Y			N		
Transport five people		Y			N			Y			Y		
Wants:	Weight	Comments	Score Raw (R)	R*W	Comments	Score Raw (R)	R*W	Comments	Score Raw (R)	R*W	Comments	Score Raw (R)	R*W
Fuel economy	22	26.2 mpg	10	220				20.0 mpg	6	132			
Good acceleration	16	10.5 sec	3	48				7.0 sec	10	160			
Crash safety	24	High Ratings	10	240				Avg. Ratings	7	168			
Carry garden supplies	27	Small cap	2	54				Large Cap	10	270			
Good for dates (16 yr.)	11	"Cool image"	10	110				Conservative	6	66			
Max Score (10xW):	1,000												
Total Score:				672						796			

Weights normalized to 1,000 total

Figure 7.23   KT Derived Process Example—Normalized.

This judgment is not final until the Other Factors Analysis is conducted. In this example (see Figure 7.24) the other considerations are noted and evaluated as to probability (P) and seriousness (S). The poor showing in recent crash tests and the poor gasoline mileage reported by owners makes the minivan a less desirable choice than the sedan.

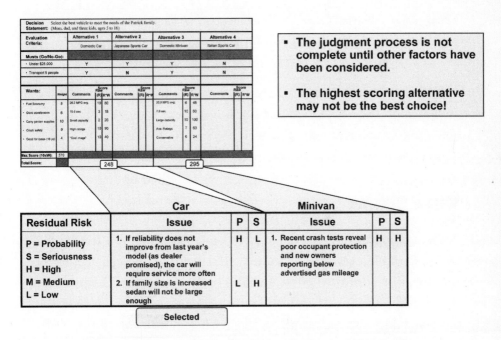

Figure 7.24   Other Factors Analysis—Example.

The KT Derived Process is now applied to our ongoing car selection example (Figure 7.25); all five remaining alternatives have passed the must criteria and those that did not have been eliminated from further evaluation. Only the prioritized, weighted, and scored want criteria is considered.

Criterion	Wt	Brand #1 Score	Brand #1 WtScore	Brand #2 Score	Brand #2 WtScore	Brand #3 Score	Brand #3 WtScore	Brand #4 Score	Brand #4 WtScore	Brand #5 Score	Brand #5 WtScore
Price	10	6	60	2	20	10	100	9	90	4	40
Seating	10	10	100	10	100	10	100	10	100	10	100
HP	4	9	36	6	24	4	16	8	32	10	40
Trans Spd	4	10	40	7	28	7	28	10	40	10	40
Fuel Type	8	10	80	10	80	10	80	10	80	10	80
mpg	10	10	100	10	100	8	80	7	70	10	100
0-60	8	7	56	5	40	4	32	9	72	10	80
60-0	8	7	56	4	32	10	80	7	56	8	64
Trunk	8	5	40	4	32	10	80	6	48	8	64
Turn radius	8	9	72	2	16	10	80	1	8	6	48
Reliability	10	8	80	10	100	6	60	4	40	6	60
Total	88		720		572		736		636		716

Acceleration and reliability scoring without applying value curves.

Figure 7.25   KT Derived Process—Car Example.

In this example the assigned scores for all of the weighted criteria are based on the decision maker's best judgment using readily available product information. The weighted scores for Brands 1, 3, and 5 are close enough to be considered equal.

Value Curves

An added degree of precision in comparative judgment is the application of value curves, sometimes called utility curves, that portray the linear or nonlinear criteria values of the evaluators that enable more precise scoring of each alternative. Figure 7.26 depicts the values assigned to acceleration. Note that it is nonlinear and that all zero to 60 mph acceleration of five seconds or quicker will receive a score of 10. There is no scoring benefit for accelerations quicker than five seconds. For zero to 60 mph accelerations of 6 seconds to 10 seconds the scoring falls off rapidly, decreasing to a score of 0 for 10 seconds and higher.

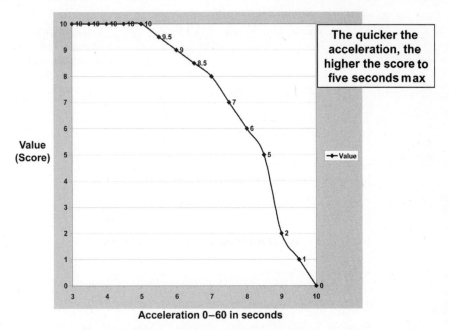

Figure 7.26   Criteria Scoring Curve—Car
Acceleration Example.

Similarly, the scoring of reliability is also nonlinear. In Figure
7.27 the scoring of reliability is based on the number of good dots
that are identified in the *Consumer Reports* car reliability reports
published once each year that are based on owners' reported
problems.

Note that there is a value (score) of zero applied to all dot
quantities from none to 6.5 dots. Then the curve rises rapidly,
reaching a value of 10 for any car earning fifteen reliability dots
or more.

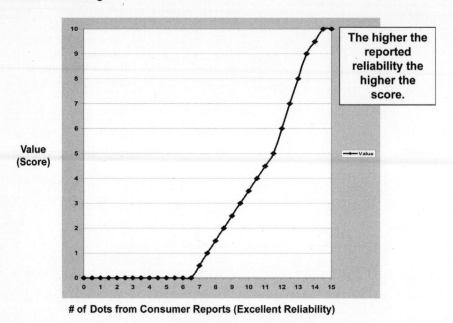

of **Dots from Consumer Reports (Excellent Reliability)**

Figure 7.27   Criteria Scoring Curve—Car
Reliability Example.

By applying these value curves to the scoring of our vehicle judgment example the results shown in Figure 7.28 are achieved.

Car	0-60 mph Acceleration	Value (Score) (from value curve)
Brand #1	7.1 sec.	7.8
Brand #2	7.3 sec.	7.4
Brand #3	7.5 sec.	7.0
Brand #4	6.6 sec.	8.5
Brand #5	6.4 sec.	8.7

Car	# from Consumer Reports	Value (Score) (from value curve)
Brand #1	14.5	10.0
Brand #2	15.0	10.0
Brand #3	13.5	9.0
Brand #4	?	TBD Insufficient data
Brand #5	13.5	9.0

Figure 7.28   Scoring Criteria by Using Value Curves.

Then when these results are applied to the KT weighted scoring matrix the outcomes are as shown in Figure 7.29.

Criterion	Wt	Brand 1		Brand 2		Brand 3		Brand 4		Brand 5	
		Scr	WtScore	Scr	WtScore	Scr	WtScore	Scr	WtScore	Scr	WtScore
Price	10	6	60	2	20	10	100	9	90	4	40
Seating	10	10	100	10	100	10	100	10	100	10	100
HP	4	9	36	6	24	4	16	8	32	10	40
Trans Spd	4	10	40	7	28	7	28	10	40	10	40
Fuel Type	8	10	80	10	80	10	80	10	80	10	80
mpg	10	10	100	10	100	8	80	7	70	10	100
0–60	8	7.8	62	7.4	59	7.0	60	8.5	68	8.7	69.6
60–0	8	7	56	4	32	10	80	7	56	8	64
Trunk	8	9	72	2	16	10	80	1	8	6	48
Turn radius	8	8	64	10	80	6	48	4	32	6	48
Reliability	10	10	100	10	100	9	90	6	60	9	90
Total	88		770		639		762		636		720

Figure 7.29   Acceleration and Reliability Scored Using Value Curves.

This outcome, based on weighted scores using value scoring curves for acceleration and reliability, now reveals Brand 1 as the highest scoring because of the high value of acceleration and reliability that provides a 12-point benefit to Brand 1 over Brand 3. Three vehicles are within 10 percent and all should be considered. Again, this is a judgmental process and excessive precision is not warranted. The final judgment can now be based on test driving the three highest scoring alternatives and applying emotion-based judgment. If all have equal emotional appeal then Brand 1 should be the choice if there are no other factors to influence the judgment.

Analytical Hierarchy Process (AHP)

While the KT Derived Process is valuable for fact-based multiattribute alternative judgment, it has a shortcoming that is considered serious by some. In the KT Derived Process the criteria weighting and the alternative scoring are determined by qualitative judgment of the decision maker without verification that they accurately represent the relative priorities. The Analytical Hierarchy Process (AHP) was designed to reduce that deficiency. As identified in Figure 7.30 AHP requires pairwise comparisons for both criteria weighting and alternative scoring to ensure that weights and scores accurately reflect the relative importance of the decision maker. This process requires increased mathematics and is considered valuable by some and not worth the effort by others.

Type	Name	Characteristics
	Analytical Hierarchy Process (AHP)	Pairwise prioritization, weighted scores, and other factors
Fact Based	Kepner-Tregoe (KT) Derived Process	Prioritization, weighted scores, and other factors
	Pugh's Process	Prioritize, weight, and rate
	Dominance Analysis Process	Compliance table and even swaps
	Rank Sums Process	Criteria ranking sums

Figure 7.30   Analytical Hierarchy Process (AHP).

AHP applies criteria prioritization, criteria weighting, and alternative-weighted scoring similar to the KT Derived Process, but more rigor in assigning both the weights and scores is required. The core of this rigor is pair-wise comparison where a nine-step numerical scale is applied to reflect the relative importance between criteria pairs.

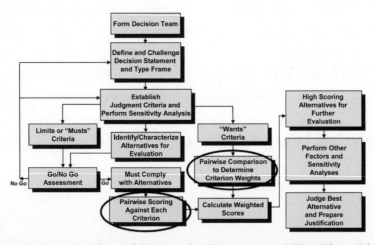

Figure 7.31   Analytical Hierarchy Process—AHP—Flow Chart.

As illustrated in the flow diagram in Figure 7.31, the process is identical to the KT Derived Process except for the criteria weighting steps and the steps for scoring the alternatives for criteria satisfaction both of which require pairwise comparison.

For criteria weighting the comparison of all criteria in pairs produces a comparison-based matrix representing the proportional mathematical relationships between every criteria pair. There are various interpretations of the comparative scale to be used to judge relative importance. A popular approach is illustrated in Figure 7.32.

Numerical Importance Rating	Relative Criterion Importance
1	Equal Importance
3	Slightly More Important
5	Strong Importance
7	Very Strong Importance
9	Extremely More Important

Figure 7.32   Numerical Ratings for Relative Criteria Importance.

If desired, the weights of 2, 4, 6, and 8 can be included for interpolations among the five defined levels.

For a set of four criteria there are $n(n-1)/2$ comparisons, or six. Keep in mind that a 20-criteria evaluation would require 190 comparisons, which is the reason that software is commonly used to handle the mechanics of this process. Note that for KT and AHP processes it is a best practice to restrict the number of criteria to 10 or less. Too many criteria tend to blur the judgment process. When more are required, structuring a criteria hierarchy is beneficial.

For our simple example of four criteria, the pairwise matrix might appear as shown in Figure 7.33.

Criterion Comparison		More Important	Importance Level Rating
A	B	A	7
A	C	A	3
A	D	D	5
B	C	C	2
B	D	D	9
C	D	D	5

Figure 7.33   Pairwise Criteria Rating Example.

To calculate the relative weights based on this information, a numerical comparison matrix is constructed to show all comparisons and their relative importance numerically based on applying the numerical rating scale (see Figure 7.34). For example, the matrix illustrates that A is very strong compared to B. That comparative relationship is shown in the numerical matrix for A relative to B as 7 and for B to A as 1/7.

Criterion	A	B	C	D
A	1	7	3	1/5
B	1/7	1	1/2	1/9
C	1/3	2	1	1/5
D	5	9	5	1
All Rows				

Figure 7.34   Pairwise Comparison Numerical Ratios.

To determine the weights and scores when pairwise comparison is applied, the following simple method is sufficiently accurate to be of benefit. The rows are summed and then the row sums are compared to the sum of all the rows to determine the row percentage (see Figure 7.35). For instance, for Row A the row sum of 11.2 is divided by 36.48, the sum of all rows. Slightly more accurate calculations are made by software designed for this purpose.

Criterion	A	B	C	D	Row Sum	Criterion Weight
A	1	7	3	1/5	11.20	0.31
B	1/7	1	1/2	1/9	1.75	0.05
C	1/3	2	1	1/5	3.53	0.10
D	5	9	5	1	20.00	0.55
All Rows					36.48	

Figure 7.35   Criteria Weight Calculation Based on Pairwise Ratio.

When pairwise comparisons are used for scoring, see the example in Figure 7.36, where for Criteria A, Alt 1 is strongly superior (5) to Alt 2 and Alt 3 is very slightly superior (2) to Alt 2.

Criterion A	Alt 1	Alt 2	Alt 3	Row Sum	Alt Score
Alt 1	1	5	1/3	6.33	0.45
Alt 2	1/5	1	1/2	1.70	0.12
Alt 3	3	2	1	6.00	0.43
Total				14.03	

Figure 7.36   Criteria Score Calculation Based on Pairwise Ratio.

Based on these factors, the weighted score for Alternative 1 and Criteria A is the product of 0.31 (Criteria A's weight) × 0.45 (Alternative 1's score, above) or 0.14.

When all criteria have been evaluated and rated against the pairwise comparison standard and the weighted scores calculated then a quantitative fact-based judgment can be made. However, as in the KT Derived Process, Other Factors Analysis should be performed to take into account information not previously considered either because of oversight or newly learned.

Sensitivity Analysis

In both the KT and AHP Processes two sensitivity analyses should be performed. The first is made at the outset to ensure that the judgment criteria are not overly skewed such that the result does not reflect the decision maker's intent. A simple way of making this assessment is to construct a pie chart of the weighted criteria and make a judgment as to the relative proportions of the weighting. See Figure 7.37 for a pie chart of the prior AHP example.

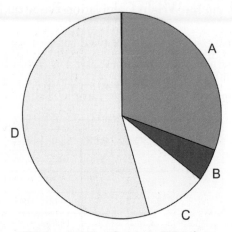

Figure 7.37   Criteria Weight.

The second sensitivity analysis should be made as part of the Other Factors Analysis to understand which of the criteria ultimately drove the selection and if in hindsight that influence is appropriate. For instance, in the selection of a family automobile the audiovisual entertainment system with surround sound may have actually driven the judgment among some close competitors. Again, that is fine if that was the intent, but in hindsight safety may be considered more important than the entertainment system and a judgment should be made as to whether safety was adequately represented by the criteria weighting.

Criteria Hierarchy

Thus far, only single-level judgment criteria hierarchy has been illustrated. Often judgment criteria are best managed in a hierarchy, with proportional influence distributed throughout the hierarchy in the form of appropriate criteria weights. For instance, an important criteria for a vehicle judgment is almost always safety and safety may warrant a weighting of 40 percent of the total weighting allocation. Safety may then be further decomposed into crash test results, braking distance, pre-crash seat belt tensioners, and satellite-based crash reporting, where each of these criteria receive a weight within the 40 percent allocation for overall safety. In that case and when using AHP pairwise comparisons, the four subsafety criteria will have to be compared to one another to arrive at the appropriate subweights to be used in weighted scoring. An example is shown in Figure 7.38.

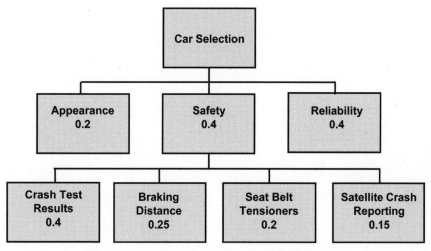

Figure 7.38   Criteria Hierarchy Example.

For this example, crash test results will have a resultant weight of 0.4 × 0.4, or 0.16, and braking distance will have a weight of 0.4 × 0.25, or 0.1, and so on.

Fact-Based Decision Analysis Software

There are commercial computer applications to assist in the process and mathematics of making team managed multiattribute fact-based

Probability-Based Judgment

Decisions in Uncertainty

While many decisions in life can be made applying fact-based judgment using information that can be researched, a significant number of decisions, especially with regard to health and future events, must be made based on varying degrees of uncertainty. There are two fundamental categories of uncertainty. The first is uncertainty that enjoys relevant past history which serves as the basis for projections and predictions regarding the probability of potential future outcomes. Internet sites provide predictions of weather, earthquakes, and even financial performance, although the latter is always branded with the statement that past history cannot guarantee future performance. The practice of using past history to predict future probabilities is called the "frequentist approach" and is based on the frequency of occurrence of similar past events, whether occurring naturally or derived by experimentation.

The second probability category involves uncertainty, where there is no prior experience or history, no experimentation results, or any other relevant information to facilitate estimating a prediction. This second type is prevalent in pharmaceutical trials and in estimating future business predictions relative to emerging technology or in gauging the success of new business tactics where no past history exists. A clairvoyant could be helpful for the second type. Figure 8.1 identifies the two probability based methods that follow.

Probability Based	Bayesian Team Support	Requires experts with beliefs, alternatives, preferences, and ongoing updates
	Decision Tree Analysis	Requires uncertainty estimates and value knowledge

Figure 8.1   Probability Based Judgments.

Predictable Probability Decisions

While the KT Derived Process is popular for fact-based decisions, the most popular process for uncertainty-based decisions is the decision tree, which expresses the outcomes of each alternative branch as an expected value or expected outcome to facilitate alternative comparisons. The decision tree is recognized as a method for calculating conditional probabilities. The decision tree method is easy to comprehend and interpret but the credibility of the results lies in the probabilities assigned to each alternative path by the decision maker and the associated comparative end values assigned to the predicted outcomes (both of which are subjective and can be seriously unrealistic).

Decision Tree Analysis

Figure 8.2 depicts the basics of decision tree nomenclature.

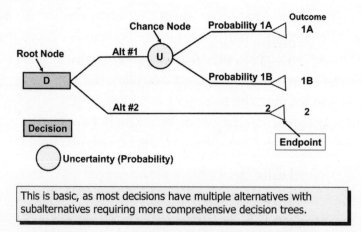

This is basic, as most decisions have multiple alternatives with subalternatives requiring more comprehensive decision trees.

Figure 8.2   Decision Tree Nomenclature.

The root node is the decision or choice to be made. In this case, the decision maker must select Alternative 1 or Alternative 2. Both Alt 1 and Alt 2 have a probability of 1. The circle is the chance node or uncertainty node, which in this case shows Alternative 1 with two probability-based alternatives designated as Probability 1A and Probability 1B, which when they are combined equals the probability of Alt 1 of 1. At the right extreme are the end points for the three alternatives offered, illustrated as triangles 1A, 1B, and 2.

To experience the decision tree judgment method the following example (see Figure 8.3) is helpful. A frequent traveler between City 1 and City 2 is torn between flying and driving since neither way is free of difficulties. The traveler finds that driving is quite reliable, but that unpredictable traffic causes about an extra hour or more 5 percent of the time. However, even with commute time to and from the airport, flying is somewhat faster, but weather can cause delays of three hours or more 30 percent of the time.

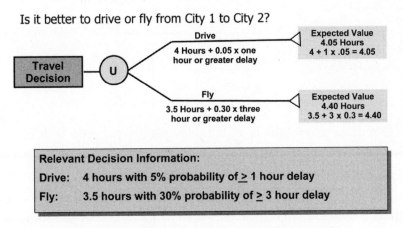

Figure 8.3   Decision Tree Travel Example.

The expected value, sometimes called expected outcome, is determined by multiplying the event end value by the probability of achievement. In this case it is the base time plus the probability of delay multiplied by the duration of the delay. For this example it makes more sense to drive as long as the probability and duration of delays remain constant. The traveler, however, may choose to make the decision based on current weather and traffic information, which would provide near real-time probabilities of delay than the longer term averages applied here.

This example is simple to solve since the value of the results are easily expressed in travel-time hours.

The next examples (see Figures 8.4 and 8.5), dealing with cataract surgery, illustrates the difficulty often experienced in assigning end values to the alternative outcomes.

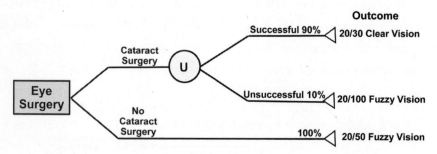

Figure 8.4   Decision Tree Eye Operation Example.

The three probabilities of 100 percent, 90 percent, and 10 percent are easy to determine, based on available medical history. The difficulty in resolving this selection is the decision maker's assignment of his personal relative values to the three possible vision outcomes. If the existing 20/50 fuzzy vision is deemed to be a relative value of 4 on a scale of 10, and 20/100 fuzzy vision has an assigned value of 2, and 20/30 clear vision is a 9, then the expected values are as shown and the selection is easily made as long as the decision maker is comfortable with the 90/10 risk probability.

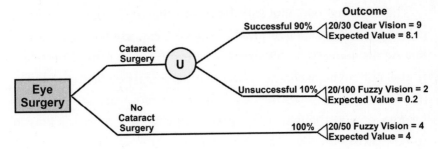

Figure 8.5   Decision Tree Eye Operation Example.

In Figure 8.6 the selection is not as straightforward. The decision is, should a sixteen-year-old buy car collision insurance? Fortunately there is abundant information relevant to accident probabilities for this class of driver and the resultant probability tree is as shown.

Should 16-year-old with a $10,000 car buy collision insurance?

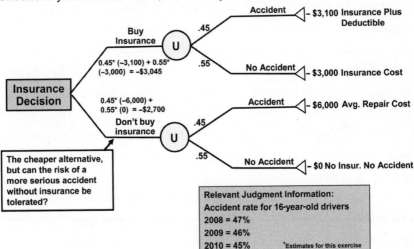

Figure 8.6   Decision Tree—Car Insurance Example.

In this case the facts are that auto collision insurance will cost $3,000 with a $100 deductible, and the average cost of accident repair is $6,000. The accident statistics are available from state records and are illustrated. For this example, 45 percent has been selected.

The expected outcome calculations for buying insurance reveal a calculated cost expense of $3,045, while the expected outcome of not buying insurance is a cost expense of just $2,700. While the selection of not buying insurance is the mathematical best alternative, the small risk of a much costlier accident usually motivates drivers to buy insurance even though in the long run being self-insured is known to be mathematically more cost effective. After all, insurance companies accept the risk shown, pay salaries, and make a profit besides.

Gambling is based on predicable probabilities and those who do well are expert at calculating the expected value of each competitive situation. In poker the betting is done based on the evidence on the table. Each hand has an expected value (outcome) and if one player can routinely get other players to pay more for the hand than the hand is worth statistically, then they have "won" against the other players even though they may not actually have won that particular hand. With this tactic routinely applied, in the long run the other players will eventually lose and the conservative player who invests in hands where the payout provides a distinct advantage should ultimately win. A player must be very good at mathematics, with rapid and accurate quantitative evaluations of each betting situation.

Slot machines do not offer the ability to bid after the competitive situation is understood, as in poker. With slot machines the player's money is invested with no situational knowledge except that the machine is designed, built, and adjusted to favor the house at some predetermined and built-in percentage rate. Roulette is similar. Roulette and slot machines are based on gambler judgments being based on indifference since others are making the outcome decision (the house).

Techniques for Reducing Uncertainties

There are techniques for sizing or reducing the uncertainties involved in the judgment of alternatives. If the uncertainty involves market predictions then market surveys, focus groups, market testing, and marketing experts can all add informed insight into projections of the future.

For technical judgment, modeling, experimentation, prototyping, and proof of concepts can all reduce the uncertainties of emerging issues. There are, however, some decision areas where the conditions of uncertainty require advanced analytical techniques that go beyond the scope of this book. Examples of this situation are outlined later, where the reader is urged to seek specialized assistance.

Judgments of High Uncertainty

Judgments based on highly uncertain conditions are the most difficult type. Particularly difficult are decisions in which both the probabilities of the occurrences of the alternatives and the estimations of projected outcome values are highly uncertain and there is no relevant history or research to help quantify these factors. Several universities provide advanced study leading to a PhD degree in Decision Analysis that embraces the available analytical techniques.

Judgments of Variable High Uncertainty

Bayesian Team Support (BTS) is a method devised to address decisions where the uncertainties are unknowable and changing. Instead of the past history-based frequentist approach, it instead relies on groups of experts who provide their degrees of belief in each plausible future-based alternative. These degrees of belief are expected to change as increased information is available about the decision and decision context. This approach has proven to be successful and now impacts our daily lives as our virus software continually learns what is spam and what is not and then eliminates the spam from our computers. Similarly, speech recognition software initially has a difficult time being accurate but then over time it makes better and better decisions until it becomes almost flawless in translating our speech to text.

The difference between Frequentist and Bayesian approaches are summarized in Figure 8.7.

Factor	Frequentist	Bayesian
Approach	Based on measurements of past events	Based on predictions of future events by experts
Evidence	Historical event measurements	No evidence, only future event belief predictions
Rules	Applied process	Updated when new information becomes available and predictions change
Decision Application	Historical evidence is used to justify judgments	Uses most recent information to adjust opinions and the strengths of the beliefs

Figure 8.7   Frequentist and Bayesian Comparison.

Detailed coverage of the Bayesian Team Support approach to decisions of variable high uncertainty is beyond the scope of this book and the reader is encouraged to seek further knowledge in books and courses specifically directed to this subject.

Group Decision Making

To this point, this book has been about preparing for and making the best judgment about choices in our personal and business lives. The models, techniques, and processes are applicable whether we are making these choices as a sole decision maker or as a contributor to a group or in a team decision environment.

When making decisions as a group there are best practices that can enhance the process and efficiency and keep the group from sliding into unproductive tangents.

These are recommended best practices:

1. *Rules and code of conduct.* These establish the decision customer, decision-making environment, decision maker, vocabulary, critical constraints, timing, and process for the decision-making team.

2. *Techniques and tools.* These define the judgment process to be used such as Rank Sums or AHP and any computer aided tools to assist such as ExpertChoice.

3. *Stakeholder RACI matrix.* The RACI Matrix identifies those Responsible, Accountable, Consulted, and Informed for the decision process.

4. *Independent facilitator.* The decision process facilitator should be skilled in the processes, but should not have a vested interest in the outcome.

5. *Validated judgment criteria.* The team developed and weighted judgment criteria should be reviewed and approved by the customers of the decision outcome.

6. *Schedule.* The time phased sequence for preparation, evaluation, and execution of the decision process.

7. *Ice breaker.* An event to bond the decision team and to anchor the critical ground rules.

CHAPTER
10

Summary

We make hundreds of thousands of decisions in our lifetime. Often we make decisions completely unaware of the basis for our judgment. Flawed decisions are most often flawed because the wrong judgment basis was applied, like applying emotion as a decision driver rather than applying relevant facts to achieve a more logical outcome. Decisions are rarely flawed due to the misapplication of a mathematical process. When you are about to make a decision, deliberately select the basis for your judgment and know why you have selected that basis.

We often make decisions without recognizing and reacting to whether they involve the potential of bad and permanent outcomes that can determine our quality of life. We also tend not to recognize the importance of respecting binding decisions and of deliberately reducing the uncertainty in probability-based decisions. If we train ourselves to increase this awareness and address these important decision issues, we will become more decision fit and more diligent and rigorous with decisions of high significance.

There are several fact-based judgment processes that can help guide you to credible and defensible selections. Credible selections can be achieved by applying either the KT Derived Process or AHP when facing multiattribute fact-based decisions where the best choice is not obvious.

As you go forward, become acutely aware of the basis for your own judgments and the judgments of others making decisions. Train to be as decision fit as possible and skilled in the application of credible judgment processes.

If you are part of a decision group and you witness the process migrating from sound, fact-based judgment to emotional or intuition-based judgment, alert the group as to what they are about to do and if necessary use the examples in this book to enlighten them as to the dangers of that approach.

Above all, teach the youth you can influence about the fundamentals of permanent and binding decisions. They need to understand these concepts to avoid making irrevocable decisions that will adversely affect the rest of their lives.

Thank you for exercising sound judgment and for making the decision to read this book.

You are invited to download a convenient wallet card of the decision type model and the decision-judgment model at www .decisionfit.com.

BIBLIOGRAPHY

Ariely, D. *Predictably Irrational.* New York: HarperCollins, 2008.

Bazerman, M. *Judgment in Managerial Decision Making.* Hoboken, NJ: John Wiley & Sons, 2006.

Covey, S. *The 6 Most Important Decisions You Will Ever Make.* New York: Fireside, 2006.

Gladwell, M. *Blink: The Power of Thinking Without Thinking.* New York: Back Bay Books, 2007.

———. *The Tipping Point.* New York: Back Bay Books, 2002.

Haines, S. G. *The Manager's Pocket Guide to Systems Thinking and Learning.* Amherst, MA: Centre for Strategic Management, HRD Press, 1998.

Hammond, J. *Smart Choices.* New York: Broadway Books, 1999.

Harvard Business School Publishing. *Harvard Business Review on Decision Making.* Boston: Author, 2001.

Henderson, D. *Making Great Decisions in Business and Life.* Chicago: Chicago Park Press, 2006.

Hoch, S. *Wharton on Making Decisions.* New York: John Wiley & Sons, 2001.

Howard, Ronald A. *Ethics for the Real World: Creating a Personal Code to Guide Decisions in Work and Life.* Boston: Harvard Business School Press, 2008.

Keirsey, D. *Please Understand Me.* Del Mar, CA: Gnosology Books, Ltd., 1984.

Kepner, C., and B. Tregoe. *The New Rational Manager*. New York: McGraw-Hill, 1997.

Krakauer, J. *Into Thin Air*, St. Louis, MO: Turtleback, 1999.

———. *The Rational Manager*. New York: McGraw-Hill, 1965.

Olson, D. *Decision Aids for Selection Problems*. New York: Springer-Verlag, 1996.

Parnell, G. *Decision Making in Systems Engineering and Management*. Hoboken, NJ: John Wiley & Sons, 2008.

Rodgers Commission. *Report of the Presidential Commission on the Space Shuttle* Challenger *Accident*. (In compliance with Executive Order 12546 of February 3, 1986.)

Savage, S. *The Flaw of Averages*. Hoboken, NJ: John Wiley & Sons, 2009.

Thaler, R., and C. Sunstein. *Nudge*. New Haven, CT: Yale University Press, 2008.

Ullman, D. *Making Robust Decisions*. Victoria, BC: Trafford Publishing, 2006.

INDEX